# Blood of the Poor

## LÉON BLOY

Translated By Richard Robinson

Sunny Lou Publishing Company
Portland, Oregon, USA
http://www.sunnyloupublishing.com

3rd Edition: September 28, 2025
2nd Edition: January 13, 2024
1st Edition, Revised & Corrected, April 11, 2023
Original Publication Date: April 19, 2021

ISBN: 978-1-955392-81-5

\* \* \*

This translation from French is based on the Société
d'Éditions et de Publications edition of
*Le Sang du pauvre,* Paris, 1909.

# Contents

# Foreword

Sed ut perspiciatis, unde omnis iste natus error sit voluptatem accusantium doloremque laudantium, totam rem aperiam eaque ipsa, quae ab illo inventore veritatis et quasi architecto beatae vitae dicta sunt, explicabo. Nemo enim ipsam voluptatem, quia voluptas sit, aspernatur aut odit aut fugit, sed quia consequuntur magni dolores eos, qui ratione voluptatem sequi nesciunt, neque porro quisquam est, qui dolorem ipsum, quia dolor sit, amet, consectetur, adipisci velit, sed quia non numquam eius modi tempora incidunt, ut labore et dolore magnam aliquam quaerat voluptatem. Ut enim ad minima veniam, quis nostrum exercitationemullam corporis suscipit laboriosam, nisi ut aliquid ex ea commodi consequatur? Quis autem vel eum iure reprehenderit, qui in ea voluptate velit esse, quam nihil molestiae consequatur, vel illum, qui dolorem eum fugiat, quo voluptas nulla pariatur? At vero eos et accusamus et iusto odio dignissimos ducimus, qui blanditiis praesentium voluptatum deleniti atque corrupti, quos dolores et quas molestias excepturi sint, obcaecati cupiditate non provident, similique sunt in culpa, qui officia deserunt mollitia animi, id est laborum et dolorum fuga. Et harum quidem rerum facilis est et expedita distinctio. Nam libero tempore, cum soluta nobis est eligendi optio, cumque nihil impedit, quo minus id, quod maxime placeat, facere possimus, omnis voluptas assumenda est, omnis dolor repellendus. Temporibus autem quibusdam et aut officiis debitis aut rerum necessitatibus saepe eveniet, ut et voluptates repudiandae sint et molestiae non recusandae. Itaque earum rerum hic tenetur a sapiente delectus, ut aut reiciendis voluptatibus maiores alias consequatur aut perferendis doloribus asperiores repellat.

     – Cicero, 45 BC (*de Finibus Bonorum et Malorum*)

# Blood of the Poor

> *"Parvuli petierunt panem et non erat qui frangeret eis."¹* – Lamentations.

> *"Quelques contemplatifs ont dit que Jésus subit la Sueur de Sang plusieurs fois durant son enfance."²* – Père Faber.

## Dedication

### TO MY ELDEST DAUGHTER
### VERONICA

May this book be dedicated to you, my beloved child. Better than any other, it is suited to your serious mind and to your soul inclined towards Suffering.

On reading it, you shall be reminded of the infinite multitude of living souls who suffer, of the children of God who are afflicted, of all the little people who are crushed and who do not have a voice to complain with.

Your father has attempted to cry in their place, to collect in a sort of *Miserere* all the sufferings of

---

¹Parvuli... eis: Latin for "the little ones have asked for bread, and there was none to break it unto them.," Lamentations 4:4 (Douay-Rheims).

²Quelques... enfance: French for "Some contemplatives have said that Jesus underwent the Sweating of Blood multiple times during his childhood." – Father Faber.

these lamentable people. You know the price he has paid for that right and in what redoubtable school he was instructed.

Consequently, my Veronica, *true image* of the Savior of the poor, pray to that Crucified One, that he does not forget me – alive or dead – in his eternal Kingdom.

– LÉON BLOY, *Paris-Montmartre, Feast of the Precious Blood, 1909.*

# Introduction

## Hallali

*(To serve as a preface)*

Here is what I wrote in 1900:

* * *

The small number of living souls for whom the Blood of Jesus is still held precious, find themselves in the presence of an inconceivable multitude, unimagined until now. It is the "infinite throng of people who present themselves before the Throne, in the presence of the Lamb, dressed in white robes and with palm fronds in their hands." These people are the modern Catholics.

Interminably they march across the prairie that lies just before heaven. Then, suddenly, one notices that the birds are falling dead out of the clouds, that the flowers are perishing, that everything is dying along their passage, finally that they are leaving in their trail a mound of putrefaction that, if anyone touched it, it would seemingly infect him forever like Philoctetes.[3]

This horror is something out of the XIX[th] cen-

---

[3]Philoctetes: one of the Greeks, at the time of the Trojan War, who was wounded by a snake bite and left behind on the island of Lemnos.

tury. In other epochs, one apostatized bravely. One was ingenuously and resolutely a renegade. One received the Body of Christ and then, without hemming and hawing, went to sell it, to help a poor person thereby. It was done, in sum, kindly, and men were Judases without any fuss. Today, the situation is something else altogether.

I have not stopped writing it for twenty years now. Never has there been anything so hateful, so utterly execrable as the contemporary Catholic world – at least in France and Belgium – and I renounce asking myself what could more surely invoke the Fire of Heaven...

I declare in the name of a very small group of individuals who love God and who are determined to die for him, when necessary, that the spectacle of modern Catholics is a temptation beyond our power.

As for what is within my power, I confess that it has been greatly diminished... I really wish that those... people there might be my brothers or at least my first cousins, since I am, like them, Catholic and compelled to obey the same Shepherd, who is, without a doubt, the Prodigal Son; but what means are there to prevent my blood from boiling, and not to let out horrid cries?...

* * *

I live, or, more accurately, I subsist, sorrowfully and miraculously here in Denmark, with no means of escape, among incurable Protestants whom no light has visited for nearly four hundred years since their nation rose up *en masse* and without a single moment's hesitation at the voice of a filthy monk,[4] to renounce Jesus Christ. The weakening of reason among these poor beings is one of the most frightening prodigies of Justice. As regards their ignorance, it surpasses anything imaginable. It has gotten to the point where they cannot form a general idea, and they live exclusively on secular commonplaces which they hand down to their children like novelties. Darkness upon darkness over sepulchers.

But the Catholics! Creatures grown, raised in the Light! informed, at every instant, of their fearsome state of privilege: incapable, whatever they do, of encountering only error, so much has the society they live in – totally ruined as it is – been able to conserve some divine unity! Intelligences like the cups of God's guests into which only the strong wine of Doctrine without admixture is poured!... These beings, I say, having willingly descended into dark places, below heretics and infidels, wearing their Sunday best, in order to kiss amorously their dreadful Idols!

Cowardice, Avarice, Imbecility, Cruelty. Not loving, not giving, not seeing, not understanding, and, as much as they can, making others suffer! Just the opposite of *Nolite conformari huic sæculo*.[5] Contempt for that Precept is indubitably what the human will has most disastrously and most completely achieved since the predication of Christianity...

---

[4]filthy monk: Martin Luther.

[5]*Nolite... sæculo*: Latin for "And be not conformed to this world," Romans 12:2 (Douay-Rheims).

I know nothing more disgusting than to speak about these scoundrels who belittle the Sufferings of the Redeemer, so capable do they seem of doing even worse things than the executioners of Jerusalem.

Many of my pages, and not the least of them, I dare say, were written to exhale my horror of their vileness and their stupidity. I have always insisted particularly on that last item which is a kind of monster in the history of the human spirit, and which I can find no better comparison to than a syphilitic vegetation growing on an admirable face. What is more, all those figures of speech or combinations of similes supposedly capable of producing disgust are a more-than-derisory insufficiency when one thinks, for example, about Catholic literature!... A society in which people have come to the point of believing that Beauty is an obscene thing is evidently a society formed by Satan, with an angelic attention and a dreadful experience...

* * *

Do you want me to speak about their poor, nothing but their poor, whom I am honored to be one of?

I met, one day, in Paris, a very fine pack belonging to I know not what bad apostle who had figured out how to vend his Master for much more than thirty pieces of silver. I have spoken about it, I do not remember where. I must have mentioned the immense and profound revulsion, the feeling of infinite hatred that I had at the sight of those sixty or eighty dogs who were eating, every day, the bread of sixty or eighty poor people.

In that distant epoch, I was quite young, but already dying of intense hunger, and I remember very clearly that I made vain efforts to imagine the patience of the indigents on whom one inflicts such defiances, and that I went away gnashing my teeth.

Ah! Well do I know that riches are the most terrible anathema, that the accursed who hold on to them to the prejudice of the suffering members of Jesus Christ are promised incomprehensible torments, and that One holds in special reserve for them the Dwelling Place of Howling and Terror.

Yes, clearly, that evangelical certitude is refreshing for those who are suffering in this world. But when, thinking about the obverse side of suffering, one recalls, for example, that it is necessary for a small child to be tortured by hunger in a glacial room so that a ravishing Christian might not be deprived of the delightfulness of an exquisite meal before a warm fire; oh! then, how long the waiting seems to be! and how well I understand the justice of desperate men!

I have sometimes thought that that pack, whose memory stays with me, was one of those grievous images that pass through the depths of life's dreams, and I told myself that that ferocious herd was, in a way – and far more exactly than one might believe – meant to hunt down the Poor.

Terrible obsession! Do you hear that concert, in that palace where a celebration is going on, that music, those instruments of joy and love that make men believe that their paradise is not lost! Eh! well, for me, it is always the fanfare at the launch of an attack, the signal for a chase. Is it for me today? Is it for my brother? And what means have we to defend ourselves?

But those atrocious people, whom the poor, sweating in anguish, hear only the joy and happiness of, are Catholics however, Christians just like him! Right? Then everything that bears God's mark of on earth, the crosses along the wayside, the pious images of olden days, the steeple of a humble church on the horizon, the dead lying buried in the cemetery, hands joined in their sepulchres, the beasts even, surprised by the wickedness of humans, and who look like they want to drown Cain in the tranquil lakes of their eyes;... everything intercedes on poor's behalf and it all intercedes in vain. The Saints, the Angels can do nothing about it; the Virgin herself is rebuffed; and the hunter pursues his victim without having noticed the Savior in Blood who runs after him, offering him his Body!...

* * *

The rich man is an inexorable brute whom one is forced to stop with a pitchfork or a round of grapeshot in the belly...

* * *

It is intolerable to one's reason that one man might be born gorged on sweetmeats and another at the bottom of a dung heap. The Verb of God came to a stable, in hatred of the World, every child knows this, and all the sophisms of demons will change nothing as regards this mystery that the joy of the rich depends on the Suffering of the poor. Whoever does not understand *that* is a sot for now and for eternity. – A sot for eternity!

Ah! If today's rich were authentic pagans, declared idolaters! there would be nothing to say. Their first duty would evidently be to crush the weak, and that of the weak to kill them in turn, when the opportunity presented itself. But they insist on being Catholics all the same, and Catholics like that! They pretend to conceal their idols in the adorable Wounds even!...

*– Kolding, Denmark, January 1900.*

# Blood of the Poor

> *"Mon discours, dont vous vous croyez peut-être les juges, vous jugera au dernier jour."*[6] – Funereal Orison for Princess Palatine, BOSSUET.

The Blood of the Poor is Money. One lives by it and dies by it for centuries. It summarizes expressively all suffering. It is the Glory and it is the Power. It is the Justice and the Injustice. It is the Torture and the Voluptuousness. It is the execrable and the adorable, flagrant and flowing symbol of Christ the Savior, *in quo omnia constant.*[7]

---

[6]*Mon discours... jour*: French for "My discourse, which you believe yourselves perhaps to be the judges of, will judge you on the Day of Judgment."

[7]*In... constant*: Latin for "by him all things consist," from Colossians 1:17 (Douay-Rheims).

The blood of the rich is a fetid pus exuded by Cain's ulcers. The rich man is a shoddy poor man, a very stinking ragtag man feared by the stars.

Revelation teaches us that God alone is poor and that his Only Son is the only beggar. "*Solus tantummodo Christus est qui in omnium pauperum universitate mendicet*,"[8] said Salvian.[9] His Blood is the Blood of the Poor by whom men are "redeemed at a great price." His *precious* Blood, infinitely red and pure, which can pay for anything!

It was quite necessary then that money should represent him: the money that one gives, that one lends, that one sells, that one earns, and that one steals; the money that kills and that vivifies like the Word, the money that one worships, the eucharistic money that one *drinks* and that one *eats*. Viaticum of vagabond curiosity and viaticum of death. All aspects of money are the aspects of the Son of God sweating Blood, by whom all is assumed.

To make a book to say only *that* is an enterprise that may appear unreasonable. It is to offer one's face to all Christian executioners who declare the rich as *happy*, whom Jesus detested and cursed. However, there may still be some living hearts in that immense dungheap of hearts, and it is for them that I wish to write.

---

[8]*Solus... mendicet*: Latin for "Only Christ is the one who, among the poor, begs in the universe."

[9]Salvian: a Christian writer of Roman Gaul in the 5th century AD.

Yesterday was the Sicilian cataclysm,[10] prelude or prodrome of many more, final warning before the threats of La Salette come true. It is said that Messina was a superb city, not far from the Pentapolis. Two hundred thousand human beings were dead by an earthquake. Has anyone thought that one hundred thousand at most must have been killed on the spot? Or one hundred thousand deaths spread out over fifteen or twenty days.

A lover of justice, I want to believe that the rich have been favored by this privilege, after so many other privileges, and that they were not denied this occasion to reflect, in the vestibule of hell, on the delights and on the *solidity* of wealth. There was talk of a woman survivor, immobilized under the rubble, whose hand had been devoured by her cat buried alongside with. Was that the "right" or the "left" hand, that hand made for giving, like all hands? Forgetful of the starving people, it may have served to feed that one single animal which, in that way, continued to trust her.

Terrible lessons, if you will, rudimentary nevertheless, but how lost on us! Much more terrible ones will be needed, and one senses them approaching... Christianity is in vain, the Word of God is in vain. Consequently, witness the "Weighty Arm" that was announced, the visible and indisputable Arm.

Ah! it is about time! The right to riches, effective negation of the Gospel, anthropophagic derision of the Redeemer, is inscribed in all the codes. Impos-

---

[10]Sicilian cataclysm: Sicily had an earthquake on Dec 28, 1908.

sible to remove that tenia without tearing out the en-
trails, and the operation is urgent. God will provide.
"You do not have the right to enjoy yourself while
your brother suffers!" cries out every day, louder and
louder, the infinite multitude of desperate men.

The present book will be the echo of that
clamor.

*– Paris-Montmartre, January 23, 1909. Feast
of the Espousals of the Blessed Virgin Mary.*

# Chapter 1: The Map of the Future

*"J'attache une grande importance et une grande idée de gloire à détruire la mendicité."[11]* – NAPOLEON.

I have, under my eyes, a nightmarish thing, a "hypothetical" future map of Europe, which could be Europe tomorrow, published by a review on the occasion of the earthquakes that destroyed Messina and Reggio. Scientifically, strictly, implacably, it is deduced or supposed that Europe is designated for inevitable and prodigious, near-term perhaps, geological upheavals.

"Our southern shores will fall away first, *until the English Channel is reunited with the Mediterranean*." All that will remain of eastern France will be Alpine or Jurassic scraps. The Rhone will drain into the department of Ain and it is at Cologne or Mainz that the Rhine will plunge into... the Atlantic. No more Seine, no more Loire, no more Garonne. A sea gulf will separate the Pyrenees from some debris of Western France. Our Brittany, ever indomitable, will be an island and, of the proud British realm, submerged like an Atlantis, only Scotland and some miserable rocks of Ireland will remain.

Italy, deprived of Lombardy, Sicily, and two thirds of its littoral, will resemble the large spine of some horrible, devoured fish. Above, Iceland, intact

---

[11]*J'attache...*: French for: "I attach a great importance and a great idea of glory to the destruction of begging."

and Saturnian in its disproportionately enlarged desert of ice; the Baltic, thirty times larger, from then on navigable above the plains of colossal Russia; finally, the Scandinavian peninsula, irrevocably detached from the Asiatic continent and soldered onto the European continent, will look like a monstrous seahorse greeting the pole.

* * *

Behold then the map of Napoleon, who did not want there to be any beggars in France and who made a celebrated code that supposed the inexistence of the poor. One has never seen that in any Christian legislation. The poor had always had their place, sometimes even the place of honor which is rightly theirs. It is why there has never been so powerful an empire for so short a time. Napoleon, alas! the most devouring and most delightful of divine instruments, the all-powerful man *with the immovable heart*, according to what has been claimed, and who was going he did not know where – he said so himself; emperor and king, sovereign master of the Occident under whom so many peoples trembled; behold it then, the map he thought he knew by heart!

There is no more Paris, no more Berlin, no more Vienna perhaps, nor Rome, nor Moscow. London, the only capital he had not conquered, is at the bottom of the seas that she thought she had dominated. Spain alone, completely in tact, has lingered on like an enormous reef, but how sad and lunar in its punishment for having been the cut-throat mistress of the great emperor! There is nothing else to conquer, O my captain, who did not want there to be any beggars.

One does not even know if there are any poor people left, and if there are rich people, they now wear their true faces of demons. It is over for your old guard and your Grand Army whose tombs even have descended into the abyss along with the battlefields and contested realms. It is over for your glory and your memory. All is over, except God, for he is the eternal Poor.

If some solitary wretches remember you still, it is because you were, in your manner, the greatest of the poor. You begged for the empire of the world, and you were refused it. In this sense, the sacred words of the Judge are applicable to you, and to you alone, O unequalled and unfortunate man:

"I was hungry for all the earth, but you did not give me it to eat; I was thirsty for all the blood of men, but you did not give me it to drink; I was a stranger as much as a God, but you did not receive me as such; I was naked with the inexpressible nudity of the first mortal, but you did not dress me in *eternal* glory; I was infirm because of disobediences to you and imprisoned for all those who did not believe themselves captives, but scarcely two or three souls if that, wounded by love, have visited me..."

Temerarious but certain application of the most redoubtable of Holy Texts. There are some men, innocent or criminal, in whom God seems to have placed everything because they extend his Arm, and Napoleon is one of them.

I still see him, ever and always, as he stood one hundred years ago, bent over the world map – the map of that time – arranging everything for Universal

Judgment, exactly like a merchant keeping his accounts. For that is the unique concern of every creature in the likeness of God: to Prepare for the Universal Judgment.

"England must disappear. The Scandinavian states will endure, somehow or another, to merge together as best they can. That will act as a counterweight to the emptiness. Prussia will return to being a maid servant at an inn, and Russia, repressed indefinitely, will be nothing more than a flea-ridden Cossack in the desert. I will stand above it all like the Ocean."

"Let it be so," pronounces the Lord.

"And Italy, what will we do with it? I take Naples, I take Rome, I take Venice, and the Milanese. I devour everything there is to devour, and I leave the carcass to the dogs of Constantinople."

"Excellent," said the thundering Voice that has no echo, "but you will not touch raggedy Spain. Its beggars are mine, and if you even so much as approach them, they will pierce your heart with knives sharper than the stingers of the bees that sewed your coat!"

*Beggary was forbidden*. He had struck the Poor from the record, and that was his *perpetual* attentat. Because God was at his disposal, he had the power to make the world in his own image. It is the Map of the future. It is monstrous and appears to have been drawn by Satan.

All the same, it is rough. However much one

might want the Poor to be avenged, a Europe without France is too infernal a thing. Even Napoleon's own soldiers, judged as they are for a century now, would protest.

"And what about us, Lord! Were we not the poor, the poor of that poor man who sent us to our slaughter, who exterminated us through endless fatigue and privations, but who made us so proud and whom we cherished like a father, like a mother, like a little child carried in one's arms, to whom everything is permitted and pardoned? He did not want any other poor than us who ate out of his hand, and we were six hundred thousand strong. Is that not enough, God of mercy? When we were dying in our last agony, it was our last cry. The great Napoleon was France for us, in truth. He was our villages, our fiancées, our distant hearths, our humble churches filled with the images of healing saints and old stained glass windows where ancient warriors represented him. He was all that for us and, in spite of the suffering, it was quite true that we gave our lives for all that. What difference did Cadiz or Moscow make? With him, we were always in France, in a France more beautiful than all the poets combined could describe."

It is not possible for France to simply up and disappear, for you to efface it from the earth. You owe it to us, our sweet France, the poor that we are – we have paid dearly for it!...

Oh! that map of the future, and the realm of Mary, and Napoleon the Great, and all history, and that sob of the dead! Where will they hide themselves then, the all-powerful barefoot one who must succeed

Napoleon and who will *realize*, in a way that no man can divine, the divine *figure* of the Precursor?[12]

---

[12]Napoleon: For more on Bloy's assessment of Napoleon and his achievement in the context of history and Catholic eschatology, see *The Soul of Napoleon*, published by Sunny Lou Publishing, 2021.

# Chapter 2: Cross of Misery

*"Terram tenebrosam et opertam mortis caliginæ, ter-
ram miseriæ et tenebrarum ubi umbra mortis et nullus
ordo, sed sempiternus horror inhabitat."[13]* – JOB.

Poverty brings men together, Misery isolates them,
because poverty is from Jesus, and misery is from the
Holy Spirit.

Poverty is Relative – privation of what is su-
perfluous. Misery is Absolute – privation of what is
necessary.

Poverty is crucified, Misery is the Cross itself.
Jesus carrying the Cross, it is Poverty carrying Misery. Jesus on the cross, it is Poverty bleeding on Misery.

Those among the rich who are not exactly
reprobates can understand poverty, since they are the
poor themselves, in a sense; but they cannot understand misery. Capable of alms, perhaps, incapable of
deprivation, they will be moved with beautiful music
by Jesus' suffering, but his Cross is horrifying to
them, the *reality* of his Cross! They need it in full
light and all in gold, sumptuous and weightless,
agreeable to look at around a woman's beautiful neck.

---

[13]Terram... inhabitat: Latin for "a land that is dark and covered
with the mist of death: A land of misery and darkness, where the
shadow of death, and no order, but everlasting horror dwelleth."
From Job 10:21-22 (Douay-Rheims).

Elegant priests: keep it away from them, Jesus Christ's bed of love, the miserable cross, infinitely grievous, planted in the middle of a mass grave of criminals, among the filth and stench, the *true Cross*, simply hideous, vile frankly, atrocious, ignominious, parricidal, matricidal, infanticidal; the cross of absolute renunciation, abandonment, and repudiation forever by all those, whoever they might be, who do not want it; the cross of an exhausting fasting, of an immolation of the senses, of the mourning for anything that can console; the cross of fire, of burning oil, of molten lead, of stoning, of drowning, of skinning alive, of quartering, of intercision, of being devoured by ferocious animals, of all the tortures imagined by the bastards of demons... The dark and low Cross, in the center of the desert of fear as vast as the world; no longer luminous as in the images for children, but oppressed under a somber sky that lightning does not even brighten, the frightening cross of the Dereliction of the Son of God, the Cross of Misery!

If only those accursed people were content not to want it! But they claim that it is not for them, priding themselves on their money, which is the *Most-Precious Blood of Christ*, to send in their place the flock of poor people whom they have bled and driven to despair!

And they dare to speak of charity, to pronounce the word *Caritas* which is the very Name of the divine Third Person! Prostitution of words enough to put fear in the devil! That beautiful lady, who does not have the decency even to surrender her body to the poor souls whom she arouses, will go, this very

evening, to show all that she can of her white, sepul-
chral flesh where her jewels quiver like worms, and
have herself worshipped by imbeciles, at supposed
charity bazaars, on the occasion of some disaster, to
fatten the sharks or shipwreckers a little more. The
so-called Christian riches ejaculating on misery!

God suffers all that, this very evening even,
which could be the "Great Evening," as the nurslings
of Anarchy say. Yet, there is daylight still. It is just
three o'clock [in the afternoon], it is the hour of the
Immolation of the Poor. The slaves of the mines and
factories are still at work. Millions of arms work diffi-
cultly o'er all the earth for the pleasure of a few men,
and millions of souls, suffocated by the anguish of
that labor, continue not to know that there is a God to
bless those who crush them down: the God of lusts
and elegances, whose "yoke is smooth and burden so
light" for the oppressors.

It is true that there are refuges: drunkenness,
prostitution of the body, suicide, or madness. Why
would the dance not continue?

But there is no refuge for God's Indignation.
It is a haggard girl, filled with hunger, before whom
all doors are closed, a true daughter of the desert
whom no one knows. The lions in whose midst she
was born are dead, treasonously slain by famine or
vermin. She writhed before every doorsill, supplicat-
ing for someone to take her in, but no one could be
found to have pity on God's Indignation.

She is beautiful, however, but inseducible and
indefatigable, and she instills such fear that the earth

trembles when she passes. God's Indignation is in rags and has almost nothing to hide her nakedness. She goes barefoot, she is bloody without, and, for sixty-three years[14] – it is terrible – she has no more *tears*! Her eyes are somber gulfs and her mouth utters not a word. When she meets a priest, she becomes paler and more silent still, for the priests condemn her, finding her poorly dressed, excessive, and so little *charitable*. Well does she know that all is futile from now on! She has sometimes taken little children into her arms, offering them to the world, and the world has thrown these innocents into the rubbage bin while saying to her:

"You are too free to please me! I have laws, policemen, bailiffs, landlords! You will be a submissive girl, and you will pay your rent."

"My rent is due soon, and I will pay it exactly," responded God's Indignation.

---

[14]Sixty-three years: curiously, Bloy was 63 years old when he wrote this book.

# Chapter 3: The Feast

*"Je suis le froment du Christ. Il faut que je sois moulu sous la dent de ces animaux."[15]* – SAINT IGNATIUS, martyr.

The best thing to eat is the poor, and not tongue as Aesop claimed, unless that be the tongue of the poor, which is *Eucharistic*, essentially. The Blood and Flesh of the Poor are the only aliments that can nourish, the substance of the rich being a poison and putrefaction. It is therefore a necessity of hygiene that the poor be devoured by the rich who find that very good, and who ask for it again. Rich children are fortified by the juice of poor people's flesh, and the rich man's cuisine is endowed with concentrate of the poor.

General Constant of the Ritornello of Breakers of the Bank, a sworn philanthropist, throws a gala for his three-hundredth anniversary. Everyone who is anyone will be there. The President of the Republic will haul his belly along with its appendages of Cult and Justice. Even the Fleet will be represented there with Commerce and Industry; and Public Assistance, clad in a crocodile negligée, will escort the Army there in its hearse. One might swear he is in Babylon.

Beneath the gleaming table, infinitely beneath it, in the darkness, is an old miner, a very old, dark chap who has never been treated to anything but coal. He has been smoked and cured two or three times by

---

[15]*Je suis... animaux*: French for "I am the wheat of Christ. I must be ground by the teeth of those animals."

firedamp. He happened to have been left clinging to a crust of bread for twenty days, between a torrent and a brazier, without a molecule of air. No one knows how he survived with more than half his skin on. It is the most laughable memory from his youth. Anecdote for salons. He is the one who maintains the agreeable warmth in Balthasar's palace. When he finishes by fire, by the earth caving in, or by asphyxiation, with neither candles nor sacraments, he will be hauled out into broad daylight only to be shoved immediately into a darker hole, and twenty others will take his place. Perhaps one of his daughters is among the pink tripe that young cannibals of the council of the presidency approach. The citizen Lahonte, former minister of the Exterior and vaunted bootlicker in all the courts, is at his post. He plays the *extra,* and it is he who will offer to the ladies the savorous *entrée* of that old man's giblets.

There are also the young and vigorous poor out at sea. That is all one sees on the Channel or in the Atlantic. They are those who, at the very moment when other bellies begin cozying up to the table, will shove off, regardless of the weather. They will keep watch and freeze, so that you may have fresh fish, O the blessed of this world, and when they go to wait for you in the other, carried off by shipwreck, a fish grown fat on their miserable bodies will have nothing more delicious to eat. You will eat them twice then. It is for that reason, without a doubt – it must be said in passing – that fish is very particularly reserved for days of fasting and abstinence, which are, among the *right-thinking* people of high society, days of supreme cuisine, days when one garnishes mackerel with truffles.

As for what is made of bread, meat, or legumes, anthropophagy, unfortunately, is less direct. Nonetheless, it is still a first-rate pleasure to be able to tell oneself that that poultry or that leg of lamb that is put down atop of some other delicacy, when one's tubes are already full, could have gone to some poor family, or to dozens of famished children who *alone* have the right to that feast but who will not receive a single crumb of it. It is true that one really has no more hunger, especially the gentlemen, after one has eaten several indigents, but what a consolation it is to know that one has soiled with one's mouth, and savagely, bestially, dishonestly destroyed the poor wretches' subsistence, that one is a robber and an executioner, and that there are probably negroes and redskins who would rather be struck dead by lightning than accomplish a similar abomination.

It would be dreadful perhaps to speak of wine. "Wine gladdens the heart," it is written, but not many cups of wine, because in the plural, on the contrary, in general, it afflicts the heart of man. Wine is a king who does not share. It is the Blood of the Son of God, the Blood of the Poor, like Money, and in a more obvious way. There must not be many cups, therefore. When one has had one's fill, one is taller than the stars, bumping his head up against the Milky Way. "There is truth in it" and, as a result, the royal angers, the immense indignations that break the dikes, the holy strength that assails heaven's keeps.

Wine is "generous" and it makes one "see God when it is pure." Many cups of wine are impure, damaging to one's energy, disastrous for one's anger. Alexander the Great must have drunk many cups of wine before he killed Cleitus, only to die of sadness after having lost all his empires. It is the choice of the world, the choice of the rich, naturally an enemy of unity, as of grandeur, beauty, or goodness. You see them, those reprobates, with their range of glasses, drinking one after the other of the wine of lovers, the wine of adulterers, the wine of assassins and arsonists, the wine of girls and despair, the wine of the Poor – the blood of Judas and the Blood of Christ mixed together!

Why did I mention Balthasar earlier? His guests are far too unbiblical. There is no way to present Daniel to them, who was undoubtedly poorly dressed. They will be treated differently than the King of Asia's table companions. They will not be spoken to in letters of fire on the wall. A Vagabond whom they do not know will undress them with a single look and their nakedness will be so dreadful that they will ask in vain for permission to hide under the rags of the least of mendicants, to feed on the droppings of the dirtiest animals, and to drink the sweat of camels afflicted with pestilence. That day then will be the beginning of a filthy deluge.

# Chapter 4: The Embarkment for Cythera[16]

*"Nulla discretio inter cadavera mortuorum nisi forte quod gravius fœtent divitum corpora, luxuria distenta."[17]* – SAINT AMBROSE.

A rich man is met on the threshold of a Mont-de-piété.[18] "What are you doing here? Clearly you are not coming here to pawn anything." "I'm looking for an opportunity. Sometimes one meets charming little women deprived of friends and forced by poverty to pawn what is most dear to them. Some cry, which only makes them look prettier. One acts like their savior and, nine times out of ten, if things work out, one is recompensed. That does not cost much and *one has done a good deed.*"

It is not known how many of these benefactors there are, who try to keep a low profile and would be

---

[16]*The Embarkment for Cythera*: a painting by Jean-Antoine Watteau. *Vide* "The Prodigal Nephew" in *Words of a Demolitions Contractor,* Sunny Lou Publishing, 2020.

[17]*Nulla... distenta*: Latin for "... no distinction among cadavers save those of the rich that stink more, distended by luxury."

[18]Mont-de-piété: French for "Mount of piety" – a pawnshop run more in the spirit of a charitable organization essentially, founded originally and still run on Catholic principles presumably. It was designed to benefit the borrower, who had the need, rather than the lender, who had the desire.

offended if one exposed them. Everything suggests that they are quite numerous. One knows that bosses and hiring managers, in commerce or industry, to say nothing of the most respectable administrations, are, quite commonly, saviors in this manner. The Anglo-Saxons are not the only ones to practice the Gospel in this way.

"You are hungry, my dear child, you are hungry for yourself and, maybe, for others who are dear to you. Eh! well, you are lucky to have fallen in with a generous man! Here's some bread, it's yours, only you will have to pick it out of my garbage can."

Jesus is on his Cross of misery and he sees these things. He sees other things, that men cannot see. He sees such acts going on into Infinity, and he sees the majestic abyss of his very own Terror. It is for this then that he suffered and that he had *fear*, as is recounted in his Passion! I do not think that the *Imitation*[19] speaks of this fear of Jesus' which has certainly exceeded all fears, but which ought however to be imitable, as with all the rest of it. The imitation of Fear that makes one sweat blood! Only, it would behoove us to know and believe that we are, in reality, divine creatures, infinitely important and incalculable, "Gods!" *Ego dixi: Dii estis*.[20] Now, we are infinitely and incalculably ignorant of it and deny it, like false gods.

---

[19]*Imitation*: most likely a reference to *The Imitation of Christ* by Thomas à Kempis, composed in Latin between AD 1418-1427.

[20]*Ego dixi: Dii estis*: Latin for "I have said: You are gods." Psalms 81:6 (Douay-Rheims).

The XVIII[th] century, in a heroic profanation of the meaning of words, spoke endlessly of *love*. "You knew it, that sin so charming..." A fetid and disfiguring art, listless and shallow, even at the point where asphyxiation begins, faithfully depicted the souls of that epoch. There are still manufacturers of starch or beef suet who are passionate about Watteau and Fragonard. Assuredly, the disgusting concupiscence of the celebrated novel by de Laclos[21] lacks the straightforward clarity, the horse trader's unrestrained franchise, cited earlier. But that is precisely what makes all the difference. They are ferocious pigs, the lot of them, but the poverty so lustfully and greedily abused by the man sniffing around at the Mont-de-piété – the Faublas[22] and Heloises[23] of those *fêtes galantes* will have absolutely nothing to do with it.

On the road to Cythera, a short distance before the guillotine where all that beautiful society of men and women made a stop over, there was Marie-Antoinette's Hamlet, when the poor queen, in a white percale dress and gauze fichu, would go to watch the cows be milked, a rustic idyll that had cost her one hundred thousand *ecus*. It was the ultimate concession. All the shepherds of France were to carry crooks and bucolically tend their sheep, decorated with ribbons, in frontispiece landscapes, while playing the flute with shepherdesses crowned with roses...

[21]Celebrated novel by Laclos: a reference to *Les Liaisons dangereuses*, by Choderlos de Laclos.

[22]Faublas: a reference to *Les Amours du chevalier de Faublas,* by Louvet de Couvray.

[23]Heloises: of Heloise and Abelard fame.

Today, now that geography is better known, one embarks on other ships. One knows for certain that the poor exist and that they are made of meat. That suffices for the table and the alcove. The destitute are a condiment, they have the culinary value of a truffle or an aphrodisiac. "Crush me that old one," says the baroness to her chauffeur, "and then *I will go on my journey*."

On her mountain of La Salette, She Who Weeps has turned to bronze. Poor queen and very pure Mother of the Father of the poor, She in turn wishes to ignore those who ignore them. Who can ignore them with a more complete ignorance than those frightful brutes, male and female, solely occupied with pouring, one into the other, the purulence of their souls, received in vain? The homicidal squandering, the inutility of money already soiled by every filth, the very Blood of the Poor of the poor whose money is merely the symbol serving for that! And the hands of the Angels poised over the claviers of hurricanes!

Have you seen, at the Enfants Assistés,[24] in a long and lugubrious hall, that double or quadruple row of benches where the little abandoned ones sit, waiting for I know not what? There are dozens of them, more or less, depending on the season or the day. They are three to five years old and they cry.

They are the disembarked from Cythera.

---

[24]*Enfants Assistés*: in 1805 a law was passed to assist abandoned children. By 1859 if not earlier, a hospice by that same name could be found on rue Denfert-Rochereau, in Paris.

When strangers pass, the poor little ones hold out their arms, sobbing. There are some who say "papa" or "mama," believing they recognize a face, and I think it is the most poignant sight on earth. Those tender ones, among the feeblest, are under the molar of Public Assistance and they will be made to stop stop crying soon. The Administration of arid breasts is responsible for drying their tears, just as the Tears of the sorrowful Virgin were dried. Their little sobs will not even develop into bouillons of despair. If they do not have the good fortune of dying very soon, they will be turned into dry, soulless machines of infernal production.

The right to innocence, which is the sovereign right of childhood, and its law of the Twelve Tables – they will be deprived of it, if that is even possible, from day one. Their white guardian Angels will be replaced by demons. When they are old enough to travel, they will embark, in turn, for a Cythera that Watteau never foresaw and that is not scented by the orange trees of the Cyclades. They will press on to Sodom, which is not far from there, and the guillotine will complete the rustic scene as before.

Behold your people, Queen with the bronze eyes, Queen of Silence and Solitude, who wept in vain on the Mountain.

# Chapter 5: The Desire of the Poor

*"The Rule of our Order prevents us from giving alms."*
– A Father of the Assumption.

*"I knew a warder who was named Mr. Desire."*

That which must, one day, accuse the rich so terribly – it is the Desire of the poor. Here is a millionaire who keeps for himself, uselessly, or who dispenses in a single minute, for a vain fantasy, that which for fifty or sixty years has been the object of a poor man's desperate wishes. In France alone, there are hundreds of thousands of them, because it is not necessary that they possess millions. Every man who possesses in excess of what is indispensable for his material and spiritual life is a millionaire, and by consequence a debtor of those who possess nothing.

No one has a right to superfluity, except the Son of God incarnate. He alone had the privilege over and above what can be said or imagined, to the point that his privilege could not be known save by revelation. "The number of blows of the whip that the Savior received, from feet to head," said the celebrated seer Agreda, "were 5,115!"[25] Several others have gone further. Now, the terrible Roman flagellation, such as it was applied in Judea, should not have exceeded 39, *quadragenas una minus*. Such was the exorbitant Desire of the King of the poor, his super-

---

[25]Agreda: Mary of Jesus Agreda, (AD 1602-1665). She was a Franciscan abbess, and noted mystic.

fluity! We know nothing about the number of slaps, punches, or spits, but they are presumed to be in proportion.

The desire of man, it is man himself, and the desire of the Man-God was naturally to satisfy all men, at whatever cost the miracle might be set. From that point of view, the desire of a rich man ought to be, at least, whatever is needed to meet the sufferings of the poor, and that of the poor man, whatever is needed of the superfluity of consolations by which the rich are overwhelmed.

Is there a single priest who would dare to preach on this text: "*vae vobis divitibus quia habetis consolationem vestram.*"[26] Woe unto you, the rich, who have your consolation! It is too grave, too evangelical, too little *charitable*. The rich do not understand that the poor might have consolations or pleasures. The idea than an indigent will have bought some tobacco or had a cup of coffee is insupportable to them. They are right, without knowing it, since the poor suffer for them. But they keep their consolation to themselves, their dreadful consolation, and what an agony, when, before expiring, by unspeakable compensations, each parcel of their homicidal riches, they will see that mountain of torments advancing on them!

*Consolationem vestram.* What inverse desolation is implied by that indelible phrase, and what desire on the other hand! The desire to have bread, to have a little of that good wine that gladdens the heart,

---

[26]Vae... vestram: Latin for "woe to you that are rich: for you have your consolation." Luke 6:24 (Douay-Rheims).

the desire for flowers and fresh air, for all that God created for men, without distinction; the desire at least for repose after labor, when the Angelus sounds in the evening. "My children, my wife, are going to die, condemned by thousands of my brothers who would save them by giving them merely the pittance of one of their dogs. As for myself, I can no longer bear it and I feel as though I did not have a precious soul, a glorious soul that heaven could not satisfy, but which the avarice of the Demon's firstborn has made blind, deaf, and mute. However, they were unable to kill the desire that tortures me!..."

An old poor woman owes about ten francs to a benefactress who says to her: "If you cannot give me money, you will give me your labor." The unfortunate woman, full of *desire* to acquit herself, works then, cleaning the house, doing the laundry, the cooking, the sewing. Weeks, months, years pass like this. Death comes. She still owes ten francs and an eternal gratitude.

The most horrible nastiness is to oppress the weak, those who cannot defend themselves. To take bread away from a child or an old man, for example, and how many other iniquities of the same sort, the very thought of which bursts one's heart – it is for all that that the rich must be strictly, rigorously, eternally reproached.

I know two of them, whom I could name, a man and his wife. They make demands of their maid, and often repeated demands – the indignation and horror of which will make her run away soon – that she throw into the refuse bin all the leftovers, some-

times considerable, from their table, meat or fish that
have barely been touched. Formal order to rip them to
shreds, to soil them with excrement and petrol, so that
no one might benefit from them, not even the dogs or
rats. Same injunction, same supervision for old
clothes. These people barely eat. Their feast, it is the
desire and disappointment of the famished.

I have spoken about the prostitution of the
word *charity*, stupidly and diabolically substituted for
the most humble term of alms. When one is not exactly a villain, one gives alms, which consists in giving
away a very small portion of one's own superfluity –
the voluptuousness of stoking desire without satisfy-
ing it! The almoner gives the other, that is, what belongs to others, his superfluity. The charitable person
gives himself while giving what is necessary and,
with that, the desire of the poor is appeased. It is the
Gospel, and there is nothing else. Jesus who gave his
Flesh and his Blood promised his Apostles that they
would be judges on earth. The apostle Judas who
*gave money* will be the judge then of those who die
without giving any. The locution *to burst,* and even
"to bust a gut,"[27] must have its origin in the death of
that Traitor and is an admirably fitting phrase for the
death of rich people.

One wishes, with all his might, that the Gospel
had spoken of a *bad* rich person, as if there could
have been any good ones. The text is, however, quite
clear: *homo dives,* "a rich person" without any epi-

_____

[27]To burst... bust a gut: "burst" in the sense of die, and "bust a
gut" meaning the same thing here (the usual figurative meanings
of "bust a gut" not intended here).

thet. It would seem high time to discredit that pleonasm which tends no less than to denature the evangelic teaching, to the benefit of the eaters of the poor.

A bad rich [person], if one is keen on keeping these two words together, is like a bad functionary or a bad worker, that is to say an individual not knowing his profession or unfaithful to his function. *The bad rich person is he who gives* and who, by force of giving, becomes a poor person, "a man of desire," like the prophet Daniel who prefigured Jesus Christ.

The Desire of the poor is easily assimilable with the more or less impure desire that one might have for a coquettish woman who does not want to give it up. No superfine experience of the world's abomination is necessary to understand, or to guess, how much suffering a man can feel for the disloyalty of a bitch who continually offers herself only to refuse finally. One has seen some very noble men die from it. The ostentation of wealth is a similar murderer, when it is not a fierce and dangerous defiance. One may exceed all measure of prevarication and give birth, every day, to a bellyful of fury against oneself; but one must not touch the Desire of the poor which is the apple of God's Eye, the Wound in his Side, from which issues the last drops of the last stream of his Son's Blood.

Derision of the Desire of the poor is an unpardonable iniquity, given it is an attack on the last spark of the still-smoldering torch, and it is highly advised not to let it go out. It is tantamount to violating the refuge of the lamentable Lazarus whom Abraham shelters in his bosom.

# Chapter 6: The Glass of Water

> *"That water, my Savior, that living water that you promise to the Samaritan prostitute, give it to me..."[28]*
> – La Femme pauvre, LÉON BLOY.

Man is placed so close to God that the word *poor* is an expression of tenderness. When the heart bursts with compassion or love, when the tears almost cannot be held back anymore, it is the first word that comes to one's lips.

That Lazarus, just mentioned, is not only the evangelical type of the Beggar whom God cherishes in opposition to the gluttonous and voluptuous Rich whom he curses. He is the prototype. That Lazarus is the son of God himself, Jesus Christ "in the bosom of Abraham" where he is "borne by Angels." He is lying at the gate of the world, covered in wounds. He would gladly satisfy his ravenous hunger with the bread crumbs that fall from the table where the rich man feasts on his Substance, but no one gives him one bit of it. It is all good, so long as he is not eaten by the dogs![29]

---

[28]That water... to me...: based on, or in reference to, John 4:4-7.

[29]Original footnote: *Canes veniebant and lingebant ulcera eius.* Despite my respect for Saint Jerome, I do not believe in the "compassion" of those animals. One knows that wandering dogs in the towns or countrysides of the Orient are veritable ferocious beasts completely foreign to our religious sentimentality. Lazarus' dogs simply prolonged his riches.

One might think that the rich man and this poor man could not be more separate. But death arrives for the both of them, and it separates them in quite another way, *like the body from the soul*, and the great "Chaos" interposes itself, a mysterious and insuperable chasm that no man has been able to conceive of – Death itself, forever incomprehensible. The rich man, at that time, amidst the atrocious torments inversely prefigured by the delights of his table, implores the [now-]glorious beggar, not daring even to ask him for all the cold water contained in the "chalice" of the Gospel, but only for a single drop of that water, from the tip of his finger, for the refreshment of his tongue, and it is on the intercession of Abraham that he counts to obtain it. He could not be any worse off Abraham objects, pointing at the abyss. "It's your refusal that constitutes that abyss. Lazarus did not ask any more of you when you were enjoying his tortures. Your inexorable *consolation* has become his, and there is nothing more to do about it."

The glass of water from the Gospel! It has become a commonplace, as have many other Words. One has often spoken of a young girl drinking a glass of blood in order to save her father, and sentimentality, the probable creator of that legend, has not failed to call it heroism. That glass of blood, which can merely freshen the complexion of a virgin discolored by the prisons of Terror, was, doubtless, for the old man menaced by a terrible death, the glass of water from the Gospel.

It gets better. There is the glass filled with tears of compassion, the humble expression of a heart trembling with love and unable to give any more, the gesture of a small child lifted up by its mother above the dirty crowd, on its way to the guillotine, and blowing a kiss to the poor queen who is about to have her head chopped off. Ah! no matter what, by no matter whom, even if from a beast, when one is overwhelmed with suffering! The poor souls know quite well that that is the most precious thing.

"I am in need of some powerful assistance, and you give me a very feeble portion of it, but I know that it is all that you can do, and this little bit – you offer it to me in the diamond chalice that is your heart." "You will have your recompense," said the Master, "and as for me, I tell you that I will be drunk on that water for eternal Life. The glass of water is so precious that even if it were given by someone who could do better, it still has inestimable worth."

You want to make me into a prince next week, and I confess that I am charmed. A crown would delight me; but, while waiting, could you not give me a fifty-centime piece which would exceed, at this moment, all my wishes? There, on the counter, stands a bottle of wine, from which I am separated by the vast chasm in the Parable. It would cost you less than the glass of water, than the drop of water from the finger of Lazarus, who had suffered all his life to have the right to refuse it. But you do not give it to me, that drop, the desire for which exasperates my ancient torments, because you are stuffed, because you have known neither hunger nor thirst, and look at us, my dear sir, on opposite sides of Chaos!

# Chapter 7: Job's Friends

*"There is no imbecile on earth who was not put there to harm me." –* H.G. WELLS.

This work would not be complete if I did not say anything about the power of money to depress and debase those who possess it, or who think they possess it. Intellectual and moral inferiority is too banal a consequence of wealth to require comment. Ignorance of poverty appears more mind-numbing than ignorance of God even, for there are the Godless poor who are not easily lead to pasture.

Laws ensure that there are rich children, condemned by birth and education never to know just what poverty is. It would be less inhumane to blind them and castrate them, so that they may not in turn produce more monsters. Clearly, one cannot hide from them that poor people exist in the world, but, as with stinking or venenous beasts, they must be kept at a distance. If a family has a tradition of good habits, if it adheres to a Christian lifestyle, the rich child will receive from an ecclesiastical preceptor the primordial teaching that indigence was instituted for his décor, that it is an agreeable and necessary foil appropriate to appreciate for what it is worth; that, in addition, mercy practiced without intemperance has the double advantage of being the fulfillment of an evangelical *counsel* and of attracting a blessing on one's capital. And that is everything, absolutely everything, for now and forever.

In this way imbeciles are formed whose

haughty face is assumed by the centenary harlot who was formerly the Christian virgin. What to say to people who despise the work and suffering of others, believing themselves to be the lilies of Solomon who neither work nor spin; what to say to dirty idlers, to sports animals, to automobile road hogs who know nothing, who desire nothing, except to return to their filth; who can do nothing, if not cast, in the form of money stolen from the unfortunates of this world, the very precious Blood of Christ, into the mud of the highways, persuading themselves that they are the first-born and the beloved!

Ah! Jesus, humble and sweet child of the Stable, why were you afraid in Gethsemane? Did not the comforting Angel present you with the refreshing vision of the future stays of your throne and altar? Why tremble, and why shudder, O Redeemer? There they are: Job's friends, your true and only friends. They keep watch to get drunk; they pray on their knees to those most ancient harlots, and, certainly, if temptation strikes them, it will not be the temptation to give all that they possess to the poor. Rest assured then, Lord, and be crucified with joy, the *world* is saved!

A harp would be needed to properly sing the stupidity and vileness of those *right-minded people* of good press and good suffrage. Nonetheless, no matter what one sees or knows, it is incomprehensible and overpowering. Whether one is a Christian or a worshiper of idols, it is inconceivable that one does not think on death, any more than on that state, impossible to conjecture, that preceded life. "For we brought nothing into this world, and it is certain that we can carry nothing out."[30] So says the Text that I do not give in Latin, out of regard for those gentlemen of sport. So what do notaries, tutors, gendarmes, bailiffs, undertakers, and all the laws mean? What does property mean, and what does inheritance or succession mean for that poor wretch who goes off, completely naked, under ground?

"You have one hundred million [francs], a breeze passes, and there you are like a worm. You will be left with nothing, but nothing, you can count on it." In the space of several minutes, beautiful lady, you will be a decaying carcass. There was, at your gate, a poor man who begged you, through your guardian angel, to aid him for the glory of God, which would have been quite easy for you to do. But you were expected at another lady's house, doubtless, and you just missed crushing that beggar under the wheels of your car. That was your right. The curate of your parish admires you, and you take the holy sacrament in your mansion, at the back of an oratory where the overabundance of your heart is sometimes let out. Servants and guests in black habit, and also some dear persons wearing low-neck dresses, pass before the half-open door of that sanctuary. Really, I do not understand how your chauffeur could have so maladroitly missed running over the poet. But, all the same, you are a decaying carcass, and you will be more and more so. Ah! if it were still possible, what would you not give to make that poor wretch content, to shut his mouth, accusing and vociferating against you? But that is impossible, forever impossible, now. Your

---

[30]*For we... nothing out*: Timothy 6:7.

only excuse, supposing that God might wish to accept it – like the poet – is that you are an idiot for eternity.

The infirmity of intelligence of these accursed people is enough for the depression of souls. If you possessed an archangel's gift of persuasion, the most temerarious enterprise certainly would be to make them understand that their riches absolutely do not belong to them, that they have no right to them, except through the malice of demons, as inspirators of the laws of this world, and, above all, by the mysterious and very redoubtable permission of God who is pleased to confront the rich with their victims, creditors, and judges. They do not understand, and they will never understand, even in hell, where the interminable blindness of their stupidity and pride will pursue them.

# Chapter 8: Worldly Priests

*"Priests have become cesspits of impurity."* – THE
HOLY VIRGIN.

"It takes ten to make a dozen," say the hog merchants.
A total of fifty worldly priests would not even equal a
single Judas, a Judas who gives back the money and
hangs himself in despair. They are frankly appalling.
It is through them that the rich are solidified, like ice
by sulphuric acid.

It is the worldly priest who says to the rich
man: "There will always be the poor among you,"
twisting the very words of Jesus Christ so as to damn
him a little more. It is necessary that there be poor
people, and, if there are not enough of them, they
must be made. "Blessed are the poor," it is also said.
By multiplying them, you multiply the number of the
blessed. And because an example strengthens the
teaching, it is fitting that such apostles be rich themselves or that they become rich as masters or by man-
aging the households of millionaires.

Jesus is on the altar, in his tabernacle. Let him
stay there. We others, the ministers, we go about our
business which is to rake in money by all means com-
patible or incompatible with the dignity of our sou-
tanes. The poor must resign themselves; God mea-
sures out the wind for them as for shorn sheep. And
the rich must also resign themselves. To each his burden: it would be unjust and unreasonable to demand
that they bear the burden of the poor while crushing
them with theirs.

If you have millions, my very dear brother, it is a deposit that divine wisdom has entrusted to you. You must keep it *intact* for your children, make it yield a profit, as much as possible, by judicious investments that heaven will not fail to bless, if you take special care not to make any temerarious endowments to a misunderstood charity. *Quinque alia quinque.*[31] One hundred percent, as in the parable of the talents. That is the rate of virtue. We will guide you, besides, most willingly, having many *pipes* in our organs. If, for lack of faith, the ventures we advise do not work out for you, you will have at least the consolation of knowing that they are never without recompense, for those of us who know how to skim the grease off the top of the bouillon.

Wealth is agreeable to the Lord and it is for this reason that Solomon was loaded up with it. The *Væ divitibus*[32] that some anarchists claim to oppose us with is an obvious error of transcription, likely introduced by one or another of those thick-skulled and seedy monks who dishonored the Church for so long. It was urgent to put things in their proper place, and the clergy diligently see to it. At the door, the poor, or at least very near the door, amid the rush, the scramble, and air drafts. It is unnecessary for them to see the altar. The parishioners in front see it for them. That suffices. We would not want laborers or beggars without headscarves, kneeling in the place of the cu-

---

[31] *Quinque alia quinque*: Latin for "five [makes] another five," a foreshortening of the famous parable in Matthew 25:20, in which the master gives talents to his servants.

[32] *Væ divitibus*: Latin for "Woe to [you that are] rich". See Luke 6:24.

rate's penitents, on the plush or satin of their *prie-Dieux*, while these ladies are relegated to the back of the nave, near the sidewalk, now would we? Fortunately, there are some parish churches, and not the least pious ones, where poorly-dressed people are admitted to communion, but only at furtive and unimportant Masses, whispered by supernumerary priests, at very small, poorly-lit altars.

There are, moreover, let us not forget, important weddings and grand funeral services to which scoundrels are not admitted. When the Apostle says that marriage is a "great sacrament," one must understand rich marriages. Otherwise that phrase makes no sense. There is nothing great but what fills the coffers. The marriage between the Blessed Virgin and Saint Joseph must have been a very small marriage. The best one can do is not mention it. Shem and Japheth were praised for having concealed their father's nakedness with a cloak. Finally, there are collections that tacitly invite the poor to depart, holy or profitable collections, final word of the purgative, intuitive, and illuminative theology.

The worldly priest is infinitely precious to the rich. With him, no chance of growing bored for a single minute. One's salvation, no matter, is assured. It suffices to *direct one's intention*. That is the crux of it. Get drunk with the intention of being sober. Fornicate with flights of purity. Be adulterous, if necessary, to better appreciate the joy of being faithful, etc. *Felix culpa.* Evidently, that catechism is not for the poor who would make poor use of it and who ought, in all cases, to be reined in for their greater good. The poor man, if Christian by his practices – what one can admit with difficulty – has the duty of fasting exactly on prescribed days and even every day of the year, uninterruptedly. The rich Christian is a hero and even a martyr, if he replaces the stuffed turkey, garnished with truffles, with the moorhen or salmon trout, in time for lent, and the worldly abbot willingly shares in his abstinence. How many other things still! But who can tell them all? The essential thing before God and before men, before men above all, is the line of demarcation, and the esteemed worldly priests trace it with as luminous, and no less inexorable, a finger as Moses used when writing the Decalogue on the Two Stone Tablets.

It remains to be seen whether those legislators "speak face to face with God, like a friend speaks with a friend." It is to be feared, I dare say, that the question is still pending. It is, in truth, greatly to be feared. As much as one adores riches, there is, all the same, a tenacious prejudice that militates obstinately for poverty. It is as if the very modest lance that pierced the side of Jesus had pierced every heart. That wound does not heal after twenty centuries now. There are countless lamentations, women, old men, small children; there are the living and the dead. All those people bleed, all that multitude jets blood and water from the middle of the Cross of misery, in the Orient, in the Occident, under every sky, under all executioners, under all scourges, amidst all men and tempests of nature – for so long now! It is poverty, that, the immense poverty of the world, the total and universal poverty of Jesus Christ! It really must count and and must be recuperated!

There are also the priests who are not of the world, priests who are poor or poor priests, as they may be called, who do not know what it is not to be poor, never having seen anything but the crucified Christ. For those there, there are neither rich nor poor; there are merely the blind, an infinite number of them, and a small flock of clear-sighted people whom they are the humble pastors of. They are together, like the Hebrews of Gessen, alone in the light, in the midst of the palpable darkness of old Egypt. When they extend their arms to pray, the ends of their fingers *touch* the darkness.

Around them, an ocean of souls, "wrapped up in the night, has gone to bed under the roofs of darkness, fugitives of perpetual Providence, dispersed under an obscure veil of oblivion, horribly frightened. Even the cavern that contains them does not keep them from fear... No force of fire can give them light, and the clear flames of the stars cannot illuminate their dreadful night... Because those who promised to chase away the fears and perturbations of languishing souls languish themselves, derisively, full of terror..."

Worldly priests, those whom Our Lady of the Seven Swords has called with her own mouth "cesspools of impurity," hate and despise those people, by necessity, from the depths of their night. As much as they can, they insult them, calumniate them, interdict them, starve them, endeavoring to capture them in the blackmail of their blindness, stoning them gropingly with their excrement. But, to speak like Dante, the poor "hide in the light."

# Chapter 9: Those Who Pay

*"I often asked myself what could be the difference between the charity of so many Christians and the wickedness of demons."*

At this time of idle talk on the abolition or not of the death penalty, to which all men since Adam are condemned without commutation or recourse to clemency, I happened to hear a preacher who spoke I do not know what about. This priest, hardly eloquent but worked up, got so carried away that he vociferated against certain criminals who had been waiting for months for the execution of their sentence, then very near. He treated them like so many "bandits" unworthy of mercy and manifested his impatience to see their culpable heads finally tumble. That took place in a famous Basilica.

From the word *bandits* on, it was impossible for me to make out anything else than an inner, dominating, implacable voice:

Look down at your feet, then, mechanical squawk box, lacking in clairvoyance and charity. Blind leader of the blind, if you can still look on that herd of scoundrels who listen to you and who enjoy the absolution you dispense, while with your mouth you scourge other, more obvious scoundrels, less respectful of the laws of money. You may not be a bandit yourself, but look at what you are doing. Those heads that are to be chopped off[33] and for which your God has suffered as much as for yours, you promise – [nay,] you hand over in advance – their blood to be drunk by ferocious beasts.

Look at that devotee with the muzzle of a crocodile whose gossip-mongering gob has devoured twenty reputations; see that penitent with the face of a famished hyena, clinging to every confessional, laborer of terror and provocatrice of misfortune, who works, ten hours a day, to confect for herself a hair shirt from the rope of the hanged; and that other one there, eater of innocences and eatress of the Eucharist, who has no equal when it comes to sniffing at hearts in putrefaction. See that proprietress, a drunkard and omnipotent, but precious and seamless, who licks her lips while thinking on the agony of the unfortunate renters who are exterminated for her stomach of a vulture and for her rectum. See the rows of bighorn sheep and tapirs, those dewlaps, those combs and crests of estimable and contemplative shopkeepers. But above all – oh! I entreat you – see those bourgeoise virgins, those *young women of high-society* aspiring to heaven, whose white soul is full of the numbers and merchandise left to this very day on account. Brought up with meticulous attention by their unmoving parents who are lined up behind them – like barrels on the quay of an entrepot – they have nothing more to learn as far as purity or arithmetic is concerned. The only thing they really lack is blood to drink, first-rate human blood, and it is precisely what you give them.

---

[33]Chopped off: at this time in France, the guillotine was still in use for capital punishment.

Ah! you are not one of those savage apostles who would say to their audience:

"A man will die the most loathsome of deaths for us. That man is a robber and an assassin, like each of us. The only difference between us and him, it is that he let himself be caught, not being a hypocrite and also, bearing his crimes ostensibly, he is less abominable. It is in this sense that he will expire for us, and it is because I have a mission to announce the Word of God to you that I make you aware of it. I am fully aware that this language surprises you, and that it revolts you. I would like you to be frightened by it. You believe yourselves to be innocent because you have not slit somebody's throat, as yet, I want to believe; because you have not forced open somebody's door nor scaled his wall in order to despoil him of his possessions; because finally you have not transgressed human laws too visibly. You are so gross, so carnal, for you do not conceive of a crime that cannot be seen. But I say to you, my very dear brother, that you are a plant, and that that assassin is your flower. That will be demonstrated to you on the Day of Judgment in a manner that is more than terrible. Without knowing it and without wishing to, each of us entrusts his treasure of iniquities and hidden turpitudes to a murderer, like a fearful miser entrusts his money to a temerarious speculator, and, when the guillotine functions, two heads fall ! We are all of us the beheaded!"

It is certain that a preacher who spoke like this [to his audience] would not keep his pulpit for very long. It is hard even to imagine the rapidity of his sweeping. But if he had spoken only one single time, he would have been able to slip a veritable word into his auditors' ears, hermetically sealed until then by the unctuous cerumen of a servile clergy, servile but full of a pusillanimous conceit and boasting, as incapable of awakening the sleepers as of resuscitating the dead. God willing, the picador would perhaps have succeeded in planting the banderilla of an inquietude into the side of some furious cow who would never be able to dislodge it ever again.

Bossuet gave a sermon on "the eminent dignity of the poor in the Church." That famous discourse, worthy in every respect of Louis XIV's meticulously arranged peruke, was not bound to displease the revelers of that "delicious century," as he puts it. "No, Christians, I do not say that you should renounce your riches... etc." It is in this way that the great bishop of Gallicanism read the Gospel.

Today, Bossuet would be forced to renounce the episcopate or to give another sermon, and before another audience, on the eminent dignity of Capital in the same Church. Everything suggests that that theme would suit him better. "... Your life is in the light, your piety pierces the clouds. Amid so much glory and so much grandeur, what part can you take in the darkness of Jesus Christ and in the reproaches of his Gospel?..." Yes, really, Bossuet would have nothing else to say. The sermonizer of kings and princes, the haughty theologian of *Uti possidetis*[34] would accommodate his eloquence and his thunderbolts in this manner. He would have to, given that he himself – court bishop and

---

[34] *Uti possidetis*: Latin for "Use what you possess." Not to be confused, seemingly, with the same phrase employed in international law.

mitered toady of a concubinal potentate – had already transposed the Gospel, over two hundred years ago.

# Chapter 10: Pandora's Box

*"Is that not right, sir, that I look like Marie-Antoinette?" "Yes, madam, the executioner made a mistake." –* "Brigadier, you are right," *a popular song.*

"Landlords need to eat too!" said a bourgeois woman after having thrown into the street a very poor man who owed her several francs. Clearly, but one does not live solely to eat. It is not enough to stuff the tomato, one must place something around it. Jewels, for example, ladies' jewelry.

One has often spoken of the symbolism of so-called precious stones, the work of subterranean fire for thousands of centuries, so says science which is not sparing in its planetary revolutions. There are thirty or forty kinds of them, each with its own legend, its emblematic signification. The diamond, for example, is the hieroglyph of death. Pointless to ask why. That is how it is and that is all there is to it. But what one is not ignorant of, what is revealed by experience, is that the diamond is a provocateur of lust, to the point of being a danger for the most chaste of hearts. Which explains, I do not say its rarity, but its enormous price and the excessive avidity of possessing it. The inexpiable war of the Transvaal,[35] which completely dishonored a great people, is the most authentic masterwork of that unleashed concupiscence, and its aftermaths can be seen to surpass in hideous and mortal atro-

---

[35]War of the Transvaal: a reference to the Boer Wars.

ciousness what the poets are capable of inventing.

Ten or twenty thousand men fed like animals are literally *encaged* within immense perimeters. Slaves of a mining company that does not even permit children to enter and embrace their fathers, the miserable wretches work without reprieve at the extraction of the diamantiferous mineral. If, tempted by the exorbitant value of the rocks and the apparent facility of stealing them, someone succumbs, they must expect appalling punishment if their masters catch them. Their blood then is added to the torrent of blood likely spilt in the monstrous conquest of that country, transformed into a colony of hell by the avarice of some bankers.

The surveillance there is diabolical. There is, O ladies, *a purging room*! When one of those more or less voluntary prisoners is freed, he must pass through it before leaving. For the poor souls swallow them sometimes, those marvelous rocks, equal in value to prairies and forests. The purging room delivers them of them. Perfumed, high-society women, proud of their jewelry, may, without any stretch of the imagination, evoke for themselves that pleasant décor. Evacuators and friskers work in their employ. The headiness of the female man-eaters and the realization of their most beautiful dreams lies in that room. Their adornment is the yield of two teams. Doubtless, blood has been shed, and it will be again, to be sure, always the blood, since the gentle tigresses demand it; [but] now there is this other thing that the most superb dogs know how to appreciate...!

Few words have been more used, more hackneyed, by rhetors, than those spoken by Tertullian about vain and ambitious women who wear entire patrimonies around their neck: *Saltus et insulas tenera cervix circumfert.*[36] A commonplace has also been made of it, that is to say, an assemblage of sounds that no longer makes any sense. Death is behind, but also behind and before, above and below, and that is precisely how that terrible Father intended his words, being delighted, together with the Church of Carthage, at the splendid despoilment of the patrician woman *Vivia Perpetua*[37] hurling herself, utterly naked, into martyrdom.

But the furious cow who tormented that Christian has changed roles. Today, it is she who is the great lady. It is she who now wears the adornments disdained by the martyr and gathered in her blood. What do the living souls of the poor, who suffer and die for her inhumane vanity, matter to her? What are they to her, the thousands of poor souls who risk their lives every day, going to look for pearls in the depths of the Pacific or Indian Oceans?

Those seem even more tragic than the Transvaal miners. That clearly touches on the mysterious primacy of those blind and tiresome but preferable globules which the Gospel declares so precious that one must sell everything in order to acquire them. God knows how closely women, on this point, observe his Word. The entrepreneurs of fisheries know

---

[36] *Saltus... circumfert:* Latin for "Forests and islands hang about her tender neck."

[37] *Vivia Perpetua:* Vibia Perpetua? If so, St. Perpetua, a female Christian martyr of the 3rd century.

it too, and the poor souls whom they employ are hard-ly ignorant of it.

There is, far away, in the wide Pacific Ocean, around the Tuamotu Islands, French territory.[38] The Manga-Reva isles, situated at the southern wing of the archipelago, had, when they were discovered, 25,000 inhabitants. Today, they number scarcely 500. The ladies and the sharks have swallowed the rest. Those poor people, spurred on by Europeans, were turned into divers. At the signal to dive, men, women, and children jump in. Those whom the sharks do not devour, those whom congestion of the lungs or apoplexy spare, are killed by phthisis, alcohol, or car-ried away by very frequent cyclones. Thus the Maori race dies out, one of the finest in the world.

In Ceylon or in the Persian Gulf, it is even worse. Every year, twelve thousand boats take part in fishery, which employs about three hundred thousand men, half of whom are divers. Many perish from the chill in the bitterly cold waters in those parts of the sea where the outside temperature is nonetheless among the hottest on the planet. The others are, more or less, sharks' prey. The water turns purple. It is the result of a diver just cut in two. Banal accident that is hardly worth the ink to report it. A modest pearl neck-lace worth sixty thousand francs is the breakfast tab of sixty sharks and represents the awful death of sixty creatures [made] in God's image, whose ghastly pro-fession barely kept them alive.

The fable of Pandora and her box of surprises

---

[38]Tuamotu Islands: French Polynesia.

that has been harped on since Hesiod is sufficiently
well known. From that box, entrusted by Jupiter to
the "first woman" and opened out of curiosity, every
evil escaped. Only, Hope remains at the bottom of it.
Tradition distorted by the poets. Rich ladies have inherited that box, and all the imaginable misfortunes,
instead of leaving that box empty as they escape, rush
in to fill it. But the height of childishness would be to
look for hope, which was the first to leave. It has
grown larger, moreover, that famous box, to the point
of resembling an Abyssal well, at the bottom of which
lies the immobile Serpent holding the human heart in
its gob, since the beginning of time.

# Chapter 11: Homicidal Derision

> *"We can do nothing for the person recommended. The budget of our charity is locked down."* – Un monsieur dans les oeuvres.

Contrary to the dusty and outdated evangelical Precept, the left hand knows quite well what the right hand is doing. The right gives or pretends to give with fanfare, while the left, placed over the heart, holds it back as much as possible. It is this struggle, whose outcome is never in doubt, that constitutes what one calls charity galas, or simply *caritas,* and the admirable effects of those so-called Christian divertisements.

One dons the hide of the poor and makes a raucous display of coming to his aid when he is three-quarters destroyed by a cataclysm. One then collects money for his benefit, which the miserable wretches hear speak of but never quite see. For one must take into consideration the almost countless, tight-fisted intermediaries who multiply, en route over the sea, like sharks in the wake of a ship carrying people in their last agony. One must also take into consideration the suppliers for victims whose entrepots of victuals in putrefaction resemble the shops of scavengers or adorners of the dead along the roads to the cemetery.

Earthquakes, fires, or cyclones make good business, to say nothing of Asiatic or European wars

or massacres that drive it higher. Business being business, speculation makes a killing. One knows, for example, that it is within the power of some honorable
group of British or American monopolizers to decree
a profitable famine at a specified spot on the plani-
sphere. In the winter of '97-'98, a well-respected
American speculator, to maintain the rise in wheat
prices on the international market, had thrown seven-
ty million hectoliters of it into the sea, two or three
hours outside of New York. That man, who thus destroyed the subsistence of the entire population of one
empire, had been given the name of Joseph, at bap-
tism or otherwise, which means "guardian of bread."
In that same epoch, others who still had their heads
on their shoulders, used the wheat themselves to feed
the locomotives. It is a simple matter of capital, arithmetic, geography, and stomach.

Then, and as a matter of course, galas, parties,
banquets, lotteries are thrown *for the benefit of the
victims*, with an eye to matters of lesser grandeur.
And ladies from several countries are in their glory,
having had the occasion to display liberally of their
clavicles and bosom. Everyone profits thereby, except
the famished. Two months ago, as I write, Messina
and Reggio were destroyed from top to bottom.[39] It is
true – or at least probable – that a transatlantic speculation was not the cause of that catastrophe, but the
aftermath amounts to exactly the same thing. Immense sums of money, according to the newspapers,
were collected. Nobody knows what became of them.
Fifty thousand human bodies continue to rot under the

---

[39]Messina... destroyed: in reference to the Messina earthquake of
1908.

rubble, while waiting to exhale their pestilence with the first breezes of spring, and those who survived die of destitution.

The Shepherdess of La Salette, the prophetess Melanie, considered *that* more terrifying than the catastrophes themselves. *The Derision of Charity*, the derision that gives bread to those dying of inanition, only to snatch it away with a loud burst of laughter as they bring it to their lips; the derision that dries the dugs, murders the moribund, derives lust from languishment and sentimental voluptuousness from despair!

Sometimes that ends badly. I have seen, not so long ago, totally exquisite individuals become, in an instant, living, screaming torches in the middle of an impassable furnace – people who "did good," as a first-class imbecile put it. They took the Gospel, opened it wide, and planted it upright, [making] a high bronze wall [of it] to protect their pleasure, but that wall, after having turned red-hot, fell on them. Shovels and tumbrils were needed to pull them out and put them to bed. Pointless lessons for others and nowise profitable for indigents who will continue to be assisted in the same way until the Day of God.

I imagine that that day will begin with a dawn of infinite sweetness. The tears of all those who suffer or who have suffered will have been shed during the night, as pure as the dew of Eden's first spring. Then, the sun will rise like a pale Virgin of Byzantium in her golden mosaic, and the earth will awaken wholly perfumed. Men, drunk with delights and mightily recomforted, will marvel at that renewal of the Garden of sensual delight and will rise amidst the flowers, singing profane things that will fill them with ecstasy. The infirm themselves, and the putrefied living, will have the illusion of adolescent desires. Stirred by the presentiment of an inexpressible Advent, nature will adorn herself with the most magnificent accoutrements, and, like a proud courtesan, she will pour heady fragrances over herself, that make one forget life, together with her jewels that have sentenced so many men to their death.

Nothing could be too beautiful, for this will be the Day of God – at last! – waited for, for thousands of years, in prisons, in *bagnes*, in tombs; the day of derision in return, great Derision like the heaven that the Holy Book calls Divine Subsannation. That will be the true charity bazaar, presided over by Charity in Person, by the redoubtable Vagabond about whom it is written that no one recognizes his ways, who is accountable to no one, and who goes where he pleases. That will really be the festival of the poor, for the poor, unexpected and without disappointment. In the blink of an eye, they themselves will gather up, without intermediaries, all that the rich can give, while enjoying themselves and much more than that, prodigiously and forever.

As for the conflagration that will put an end to the gala, there is not a creature, not even an arch-angel, who could say a single word to prevent it.

# Chapter 12: Jesus Christ in the Colonies

*"... [He] descended into hell."* – Symbol of the Apostles.

The subject is more serious than words can express.

"Great Lady," said Christopher Columbus to Isabel, in Verdaguer's *l'Atlantide*, "give me ships and, when the hour comes, I will give them back to you with a world in tow." He obtained them, those small ships, fragments of which could have been kept like priceless treasures, their wood being the most precious on earth, after that of Christ's Cross, and for the same reason. He obtained them, as one knows, after eighteen years of supplication, in all the countries of Europe, and that was the *death* that he brought to the Amerindian world, in his ineffably paternal hands.

They changed his mission from day one. They turned his light into utter darkness, and what darkness! They got drunk on the blood of his innumerable children, and what remained of that blood, what the jackals of pillage and the dogs of vomiting no longer wanted, they gathered it up into the hollow of their hands, into the spades of miners, into the bailers of boatmen, into the cups of debauchery, into the two pans of prostituted justice, into the chalices even of holy altars, and they splattered themselves with it from head to foot! They constrained that amorous Dove to trample, like a crow, in the cesspit of assassins. The orgy of greedy and sanguinary men enveloped the mountain of his supercilious spirit like a whirlwind of tempests, and it was a most incredible solitude on that pile of sorrows!

Christopher Columbus had asked that no Spaniard set foot in the new worlds unless he were definitely a Christian, putting forward the veritable purpose of that enterprise which was "for the growth and glory of the Christian religion." Prisons and galleys were emptied. Crooks, perjurers, forgers, robbers, panderers, and assassins – they were the men charged with setting the example of Christian virtue in the Americas. He himself was accused of all their crimes, and the hideous riffraff who were sent to him were allowed to testify against that angelic Pastor who wanted to defend his flock, whose principal infamy was having attempted to do away with the freedom of pillage and the cutting of throats.

He was dispossessed finally, expropriated of his mission and, for several years, could see, his hands bound and powerless, the destruction of his work. His illegitimate and greedy successors immediately replaced his Paternity with the Ergastulum, and his peaceful evangelization with the cruel system of *repartimientos*,[40] which was the death sentence for those unfortunate peoples.

Such was the dawn of European colonization in modern times. Nothing has changed for four centuries. The only difference – extremely appreciable, to be honest – is that at the precise moment of the discovery of the New World there was a man, great like

---

[40]*Repartimientos*: Spanish for "a partitioning or distribution" of slaves (in this case).

the Angels, immolated by the multitudinous riffraff; and that immediately after him there was nothing but riffraff.

Ah! the evangelization of savages, the dilatation and growth of the Church in them, things so passionately desired by Christopher Columbus – how far we are from it! Not even a semblance of rudimentary equity, not a shiver of human pity merely for those poor wretches. It is enough to make one tremble from head to foot to reflect that the beautiful Amerindian races, from Chili to the north of Mexico, represented by many tens of millions of Indians, were *entirely exterminated*, in less than one century, by their Spanish conquerors. That is the ideal that can never be imitated again, even by England, so colonizing as she is however.

There are moments when the things that happen are enough to make volcanoes vomit. One has seen it happen, in Martinique and elsewhere. Only, the progress of science prevents understanding, and the horrors do not stop for a single minute. To talk only about the French colonies, what a clamor if the victims could cry out! What howlings, hurled from Algeria and Tunisia, favored, sometimes, by the carcass of the President of our beloved Republic! What sobs from Madagascar and New Caledonia, from Cochinchina and Tonkin!

For as little as we follow in the apostolic tradition of Christopher Columbus, where the means exist to offer something more than a volley of grapeshot to the butchers of indigenous peoples, incapable, the butchers, in France, of bleeding the least pig, but who, now magistrates or sergeant-majors in the most distant districts of the Americas, tranquilly quarter men, cut them to pieces, grill them alive, feed them to red ants, inflict on them nameless torments, in order to punish them for having hesitated to hand over their wives and last cents!

And that, – it is arch-banal, known the world over, and the demons who do these things are highly respectable men decorated with the medal of the Legion of Honor, who have no need for hypocrisy even. Returning to France with their lovely profits, sometimes with a vast fortune, accompanied by a long rivulet of black blood streaming behind them or at either side, in the Invisible – eternally; – at most, they have crushed a few bedbugs in "bad places" by the time they arrive in France, great conquerors, and prospective mothers-in-law, dazzled at the sight of them, offer up their virgin daughters.

I have before me documents, that is, such and such cases. Millions could be added to them. The history of our colonies, above all in the Far East, is nothing but grief, unbounded ferocity, and unspeakable turpitude. I have read stories to make the stones weep. But it is enough to cite the example of that poor honest fellow who had undertaken the defense of some Hmong villages horribly oppressed by the administrators. His case was immediately dealt with. Seeing him without support, without patronage of any sort, they laid simple traps for him that generous people are infallibly taken in by. They led him, as if by the hand, to violent acts charged with rebellion and *voilà*: it is twenty years now that he agonizes in a *bagne*, if even alive anymore. I will speak one day with more force and precision about that naïve man who believed in the laws.

It is an article of faith that Jesus, after his last breath, descended into hell to bring back the suffering souls whom only he could deliver. Every divine thing being perpetual, it is always the same unique hope then for the same infinite desolation. But it is truly unique, and there is, above all – I want to tell the colonies – nothing to hope for from men.

Official reports or banquet speeches are masks over terrifying muzzles, and one can say with certitude and without [need for] documentary evidence that the condition of uncivilized autochthones, in all conquered lands, is the final degree of human misery visible on earth. It is the very image of Hell, so far as it is possible to imagine that Empire of Despair.

Every Christian departing for the colonies necessarily bears the Christian imprint with himself. Whether he likes it or not, whether he knows it or does not know it, he has on himself the mark of Christ the Redeemer, the Christ who bleeds for the poor, the Christ Jesus who dies, who harrows hell, who rises [from the dead], and who judges both living and dead. He is, that Christian, he too, and no matter what he does, a Christopher,[41] like Columbus, but a Christopher with the head of Medusa, a Christopher of horror, of howlings, of twisted arms; and his Christ has been, midway along the path, annexed by demons.

---

[41]Christopher: in French, from Latin, Christopher means literally, etymologically, "Bearer of Christ."

The good young man raised by good Fathers, and filled with saintly intentions, piously embraces his mother and his younger sisters before departing for distant lands where he will be *permitted* to soil and torture the poorest images of God...

It is in this way that the work of the gentle Dove of the XV[th] century continues, and it is in this way that the Savior of the world is brought to the colonies.

# Chapter 13: Those Who Do Not Want to Know Anything

*"The executioner is the cornerstone of the social edifice."* – JOSEPH DE MAISTRE.

"Manager, sir, my properties ought to bring me, all told, six hundred thousand francs. You will any more than that into your pocket, but I do not want to know anything about it. I ask that neither my name nor my address be divulged to any of my tenants, without exception. Objections or complaints are odious to me, and I like to live in peace. See to it."

The manager is a clever fellow and has no interest in making himself liked. All is for the best. The landlord has clean hands, like a good Pilate, and his responsible agent has free rein. The one will have the peace he insists on, the other the eventual profits, perhaps enormous, that he desires. Good arrangement for the both of them.

Judge for yourself what might become of the poor under such a steward's talons. For there will always be the poor among us, even under the appearances of wealth; and those shiny, well-furnished poor over there are not to be despised. It is the profitable flock wherein the astuteness of a good mercenary always finds the occasion, in the four shearing seasons, to strike at some merinos wounded in the turnstiles. A sudden increase [in rent] following well-calculated acts of viciousness can yield the [desired] result. Mobilization of the bailiff, the sale at a reduced price, and the secret buyback of seized furniture[42] sometimes yields very appreciable profits. There are other schemes as well. But one needs a bridle on the neck and the strategic swiftness of a man of war.

The advantage is less with small tenants who are needy and without means, uncircumcised workers and fast-livers whose money each week must be caught on the fly, accompanied by slaps sometimes and always by maledictions. With this rabble, truth be told, the courtesies are fewer, and the risks fructuously counterbalanced by the discreet handling of a naïve, often exploitable prostitution. But the case of great landlords lodging scoundrels is rare, the latter being only too happy really when barracks or pigsties in suburban quarters are built for them.

This sort of prey is left to small landlords, entrepreneurs who made their fortune in construction rubble or domestics turned rentiers by dint of scraping saucepans. They have no managers. They collect the money and [give] the slaps themselves, and they practice another manner of knowing nothing. It is their firm resolve ostensibly to prefer their tripe to anything else under the sun. The ferocity of these animals is too well known to need mentioning. However, as it tends towards the infinite, they themselves who have experienced it most severely do not know what it is in

---

[42]sale and buyback: the tenant's sale of furniture to a third party at a reduced price to pay the increased rent, and then its buyback secretly by the manager who turns around and resells it to someone else at a higher price.

reality. What degree of glacial mercy were you hop-
ing for, for example, from an individual who has
spent forty years selling something for 2 or 3 francs
retail what cost him 0 francs 50 centimes wholesale,
or from this other one, monstrous among the hideous,
who was at one and the same time informer, buyer of
IOUs from the Mont-de-piété, poisoner on the zinc,[43]
and manager of a house of prostitution inherited from
madame his mother. The heart shudders to think of
these people, justiciables, who have the power to sentence entire families to death and who use it, every
chance they get, under the protection of the law.

One needs to have been poor oneself to know
what it means to give continually the best fruit of
one's labor and toil, the flower of the blood of one's
children, in order to swell the pockets of a lazy para-
site, great or small, one of the damned among God
and men, incapable even of the intestinal gratitude of
a dog for those who, such as they are, fill his guts. For
they are uncountable, the poor folk who work and
who fast in order to pay the landlord, in order to have
a defective and sordid shelter, with neither air nor
light, the sight alone of which is enough to make one
feel disgusted with life. One needs to have seen them
suffer, the little tots extenuated by privations simply
to appease the plethoric pimp whom the laws honor
and who is one of five or six hundred thousand lords
and masters who have replaced the high barons of an-

---

[43]Poisoner on the zinc: counters in Parisian bars were often
covered in zinc in the Belle Epoque and later. The reference to
poison is perhaps a reference to unscrupulous manufacturers of
absinthe, who cut the liquor with cheaper, but more harmful,
substances, thus accounting for the fate of the character
Coupeau in Zola's *l'Assommoir*.

cient France who had shed their blood to defend their
laborers!

If, at least, at that appalling price, the poor
man were assured of his shelter; if, by dint of paying
and suffering, he earned his keep finally, like the
worn-out horse that a pitiful master leaves in the stable to die! But the dwelling must yield a good return.
"In business, there is no place for feelings," no ifs,
ands, or buts. Upon the least delay in your rent pay-
ment, clear out for another shelter and good luck if
you are ill or maimed. One sees these unfortunate
wretches who have paid five hundred times [its
worth] for the lowly dream of a sufficiently sheltered
deathbed, and who go to die of despair on the thresh-
olds of hospitals. The landlord has his right, his belly,
his habits, and it is quite simple that others should
suffer so that nothing might change that. He does not
want to know anything beyond that, and the crucifix-
ion of the God of the Poor is one very old joke!

But what am I saying? It is not enough to pay.
In fact, it means nothing at all, unless one pays *in advance*. Having clearly become kings of this world, the
bastards have come up with that. If the mule succumbs before having been grimped up the mountain
of due rent, it is no skin off their noses, so to speak.
They need only push him over the edge and into the
ravine, others will follow. As for those who cannot
pay in advance, and they are the majority, there are
sidewalks and avenues to stroll down.

But that is not all. Even by paying in advance,
a young couple must promise not to have children,
and the landlords make them sign, at the same time as

the rental agreement, a notice to quit, completely legal, and on which there is no going back, in the event of pregnancy. The inert sensualist needing to grow fat like a pig – reparations and taxes, everything is passed onto the galley slaves, it goes without saying. If there is any litigation – which is hardly something to fear from the poor – the judge of the peace, ever faithful to his mission, divides the pear in favor of the brute, and society triumphs.

Two years ago, on November 9, 1907, to be exact, the Syndical Chamber of Real Estate Properties of the City of Paris, in an appeal to artists (!) arranged a competition for "the composition of a diploma or a medal or plaque" (!) to be awarded as recompense to deserving tenants, concierges (!!), etc., *to all those, in general, who might render service to landlords* (!!!). The cynicism of that printed humbug, sent to every artist, was unprecedented. Everyone may judge for themselves by these several lines: "*The matter is not unworthy of treatment, for Ownership represents the noblest thing in the world*: WORK (!!!!!), Economy, Foresight, Construction, with all the arts that embellish it: Architecture, Sculpture, Painting, etc. The field is vast and the imagination of competitors in this artistic tourney (!) will have only the trouble of the choice of figures and attributes... etc."

I do not know how this farce ended. I doubt they would have found an artist or so-called artist so far gone in general paralysis as to compete in it. But it seems to me that it will be hard to find a greater example of insolence in stupidity.

I know sufferers, dreamers, who say that, all

the same, each man should have a roof over his head and, maybe also, given that the earth is vast, a modest plot to cultivate. These good fellows are not familiar with economic science. They ignore the mechanism that is so profitable to some, to the point of believing that everything ought to be held in common, as in the early days of Christianity. Revery so little conformant with reality which sees *priests who are landlords* and more implacable than others. You heard that right, O Jesus! PRIESTS WHO ARE LANDLORDS! If you should return to this world, you would need to pay your rent *in advance* – even before incarnating – to such a canon, or the domestic of an Archbishop, who might say to you that "in the holy Name of God" he has the law on his side, and that, being a Savior of landlords, it is fitting that he should set a good example to their galley slaves. If you should have nothing else to offer than the Adoration of the Shepherds or the wood of your Cross, you will indubitably and very promptly be thrown out, have no doubt about it. Expelled by those who call themselves your servants, or with their plenary absolution.

Small or great, they do not want to know anything, not the atrocities they cause to be committed nor the most appalling iniquities, sometimes, which they are themselves the agents of. The tears they cause to flow, they do not wish to see them; the deep sobs or the cries of despair caused by their greed, they do not want to hear them. If men become robbers or murderers, if women prostitute themselves and prostitute their children, all those things are foreign to them, and must not alter, in any way, shape, or form, their serenity, so long as the money for rents due is collected to the centime and on time. With some of them, the practice of the sacraments serves merely to harden them more, while propping up – granite columns of an immunity from on high – their egoism of cannibals. Parish societies or brotherhoods of "Christian landlords" exist. They prepare in this way, for themselves, future and permanent residences where nobody will be tempted to follow them. God have pity on the unfortunate souls who live under their roofs!

The modern landlord is a bizarre being whose habit alone prevents seeing the real monstrosity. Born of a legal fiction, essentially supernumerary and parasitic, but the constant invoker of the lofty principles of Order and Justice, the landlord is precisely the most redoubtable enemy of the Family, such as Christianity constituted it. The touching and sweet word *hearth* no longer means anything. The furniture mover's ledger has replaced the *Family Ledger* of ancient France's patriarchal families. The good, old walls of yesteryear, witnesses for several generations to the joys or sorrows of beings issued from the same blood, and worshiping the same God, no longer exist or no longer belong to anyone, because the landlord himself is nothing but an uncertain larva, a nightmare that changes and that wanders about accompanied by notaries and undertakers. Your dear furniture, if you still have any, "polished over the years," is handled and sullied by vile hands, with each change of domicile. But who today possesses whatsoever it might be and, soon, who can boast even of a tomb in a determined place, now that the earth, as one might believe, grows tired of carrying so locomobile a generation?

The poor are driven away from city centers, just as one would keep the blood from flowing to the heart. If God allows the consummation of that suicide, it will be the end of landlords themselves, the end of both rich and poor, the end of everything and the beginning or middle of the universal rotting carcass. The Spirit of God will be borne over the waters of a liquid humanity...

All the same, there will be this: "You did not want to know anything, fair lady, you, who are full of worms; and you, her worthy spouse whose carcass asphyxiates eagles hovering in the sky, you also, you did not want to know anything. Eh well, my dears, it is just the contrary. You will know everything in a thousandth of a second. Your science, horribly universal, horribly irreparable, will be quite simply the Eye of God, the gaze of the Eye of God, throughout all eternity!"

# Chapter 14: The Little King

*"I saw, in the cradle, an infant crying and dribbling, and around him were old people saying to him: Lord! and who, kneeling, worshiped him. And I understood all man's misery."* – Words of a believer.

One evening, at a public gathering, in 1869, I heard this citation from Lamennais made by a sad young man who today is among the ghosts, and the bitterness of it has remained profoundly with me. I think that there are still those king-like children somewhere, and I am certain that there exists many of those old men, above all in the republican world. In any case, there are infant landlords.

Here is one who sleeps in his white and pink cradle, wrapped in lace and satin. He resembles a flower on top of flowers. It is innocence and beauty. He is called: "Little king, adored treasure," and he possesses, in effect, many millions. He is an orphan. His mother died while bringing him into the world, and his father followed her closely thereafter, one does not know why. Both one and the other have gone away, completely naked, to give an account of themselves. He has a tutor full of prudence and many carnivorous managers who take care of his affairs. It is the start of a beautiful life. If one does not kill him with gentleness and caresses, he will be a famous man in fifteen or twenty years.

His education, in any case, is assured. Nothing

will be lacking.[44] Before he will have even learnt how to speak, he will have been made to understand that wealth is the only good and that he is, precisely, the possessor of an immense fortune. At a very early age, he will know that, being the son of his father who was an admirable thief, he has a right to the deepest respect and to the unanimous adoration of other mortals, if anyone can believe however that he is mortal himself. Without risking meningitis, he will divine that this right, conferred on him by the possession of money, infinitely surpasses all efforts of intelligence and that it is ridiculous to overwork oneself.

If his education is done right, his contempt of poverty will be his torch, his light to be shined on everything, to discern everything by, to untangle everything by. And that will last his entire life, barring a miracle. If he lives to a hundred, he will never know that poor people are men like himself and who suffer. Otherwise, where will he get the idea of suffering?

---

[44]Original footnote: Certain religious have provided for him. The Dominicans, among others, have, in Paris, a school for the exclusive use of young rich men called to shine in the world. These laicized Fathers are men of sport and noble bearing. A rigid rule, in this religious school, demands that religion is *never* spoken of to the students. If one of them speaks impieties, it is inappropriate to impose silence on him, even less to reprimand him. On Sundays, a rapid mass, merely for form, just what is needed to save Saint Dominic. Occasion, for the little masters, to get together during the Holy Sacrifice of the Mass while reading filth. Sunday afternoons, vespers at the Circus, at the Cinema, in diverse theaters that the teachers lead them to. But they prefer boxing, races, and dance which fatigues their brain less, and one encourages them in it willingly. Pointless to add that abstinence and fasting are severely prohibited. As for mores, one presumes that they put fear in the horses groomed for equitation. That establishment is recommended to rich and ambitious families for a distinguished education for their children.

That idea is like milk; one must get it from one's mother's breast. One must have been breast-fed, rocked by Grief, by the true grief of poverty. Upon his having passed the age of reason, which is said to be seven years old, there is almost no more opportunity to teach him what suffering is. If some accident should force him into it – because wealth, however divine it may be, is not the water of the Styx that gives invulnerability – one does not see any other resource than to kill oneself like a cleaned-out gambler or to moan cravenly while wallowing in one's filth. While awaiting his destiny, however it might turn out, various sports will take the place of intellectual culture, which is so perfectly useless for men of the world, and moral culture principally, necessary only for flunkeys and some ambitious croupiers. Leaving far behind him those who do not want to know anything, he will not even know that there is something to be ignorant of. Mechanical sensualist to his dying day, poverty will be as unknown to him as mystical theology or universal history, and, when death wakes him from his imbecilic dreams, he will need to wipe his eyes with burning shards of glass so that he might notice finally that companion of Jesus Christ!

That moment is far off, let us hope. Today, here he is in his cradle. He could be on the street, in a pile of garbage, like so many wee ones who have been abandoned. But there is a law promulgated by demons that wants certain children to be born rich and others to be born poor.

"Your father, O little king, appropriated for himself the subsistence of a large number of people. It is right that you should profit thereby and that the children of fathers who have not robbed anyone should suffer for you. That is strict justice, all the notaries will tell you so. When one serves you your breakfast respectfully in your little warm bed, other children your age, half naked and who are hungrier than you, will search in the garbage for some precious crumbs that you disdain, if the dogs had enough kindness to leave them. But no one will tell you that because it would disgust you, my dear angel.

Any less will one tell you that those miserable children who so little resemble you have been put out on the street by you or at least for you and in your name, for you were their Landlord, and because the pretty cup from which you drink your hot chocolate represents much more than the price of the humble family table where they eat their meals each day with their parents, provided you had not forced them to sell their furniture. It is even probable that one will never tell you about it. What good are those repugnant ideas that are not suitable for you? They would laugh, your tutor and fat notary, if one told them that there is perhaps a malediction in each of the folds of your curtains and that between the two of them they place on you a tomb heavier than the pyramids of the desert!

It is in this way that human laws, frightening echos of God's Justice, make the children of the rich pay for the iniquities of their fathers. What can the Bethlehem Stable and the mystery of the Holy Infancy mean for those little beings demeaned and denatured by riches, from the time of their entry into this horrible world that their presence makes appear more horrible still? *Persecutive innocence!* Can something more grievous be imagined? A more disarmed child, made into, without his knowing it, a vase of injustice and cruelty, in whose name awful acts are legally perpetrated which he will never be able to repair, and on whose head is accumulated hatred, envy, fury, the desperate maledictions of a multitude, with intent! The Gospel says: "Woe unto the rich!" Imagine the power that that Phrase has on a new-born child?...

Yes, Bethlehem in that whirlwind of hell!... Supposing an infinitesimal religious upbringing, what might the little king think, if not that the people of Bethlehem were quite right not to take in so poor a family, and that Mary's Child should consider himself too lucky not to have been repulsed by the ox and ass and to have received gratuitously the hospitality of those animals? The Holy Family, at that time then, would have been, maybe, in his debt, like so many others, and the intendants of his wealth would have enforced it, however holy the family might be, without further ado, in virtue of the just laws that protect him, and which the Son of God himself, submissive to Caesar, could not ignore nor be unaware of. As for the Magi, or Three Kings, it is all too evident that they had acted without counsel and that their presents would have been better placed at the court of Herod, with whom they made the blunder of having fallen out with, which by consequence caused the death of many children, worthy of interest, whose parents must have had money invested in the life insurance companies of Judea.

That comprehension of the Gospel and reli-

gious Verity is, in the soul of the innocent little massacred kings, like the fœtus in the amnion, and it
hardly delays their growing up to become living monsters. Consequently, one can believe that their
guardian angels have left them, and that the sky
weeps.

# Chapter 15: Eternal Darkness

*"Et factæ sunt tenebræ horribiles."*[45] – Moses.

There is, on the top of Montmartre, a painter of wild yet gentle temperament, like the Good Shepherd's sheep. Without a second thought, he throws the rich out of his studio and shares what he earns with those poorer than himself. Also, he is not on a path to fortune and honors. Too much probity in art and no connections to speak of. He is what his go-getter and careerist colleagues call, amongst themselves, a failure.

A gentleman shows up one day, climbing out of an automobile. Curiosity on the one hand, hope on the other. The visitor has time to waste. They are so amusing, these artists' studios are, and one can sometimes meet little models there! The visited artist, whom his landlord torments, would really like to sell him a painting or two. Nothing more banal. But, that morning, the poor painter is particularly somber and the noise of the automobile gets on his nerves. However, a conversation is struck up, which is quite stupid and all over the map. All of a sudden, one knows not how or why, the gentleman, giving in to that obscure interior motive that brings assassins to confess everything, declares that he is a *millionaire*. No more need be said. The artist leaps up.

"You are a millionaire," he cries. "What have

---

[45]*Et factæ... horribiles*: Latin for "and there came horrible darkness...." Exodus 10:22 (Douay-Rheims).

you come here for? You are a millionaire, you have
one of those hideous cars that I execrate, and you
don't employee it solely to drive, from morning to
evening, to the assistance of the poor! You understand what I'm saying, to the assistance of the poor
who have been entrusted to you to their misfortune
and who wait on you while weeping. But then, you
are a despicable scoundrel, a robber of the poor! For
in the end that money that cost you nothing but the
shame to receive it from a father who was probably a
bandit – you owe it all to indigents and you cannot
hold on to it without being the most cowardly and
abominable rascal... Ah! you will not leave here without having heard me out. You have come here just
like that, an amateur, to amuse yourself on the misery
of a proud artist who would fill you with honor by
inviting you to wipe the mud off his shoes, probably
even in the base hope of taking advantage of his distress! It is only right that you should hear me out,
whether it please you or not. I repeat, you are a
scoundrel, a coward, and a dirty rascal, infinitely beneath burglar-murderers who, at least, risk their skin
or their liberty. You operate ignobly with the com-
plicity of gendarmes and magistrates. The money,
whose sack you are, which your father left you or
which you yourself stole – you have the duty to restitute it to your victims and you know it quite well, if
you are not an imbecile. But, supposing that you were
the legitimate possessor of it – which is impossible
and contrary to reason – an atom of conscience would
compel you to get rid of it. Money is for the Glory of
God, make no mistake, and the Glory of God is in the
midst of the poor. Every other usage that one can put

it to is prostitution and idolatry. But, above all, it's a theft. There is one and only one way not to rob others, and that is to divest oneself of it. This kind of talk is new to you, eh? One does not talk like this in your circle of cretins and loafers. No matter! it does me good to speak about these things and to make you hear them. For your benefit, I wish you ruin and misery. You will know then what money is. Until then, you will remain a brute. If I had the misfortune of becoming rich, Mr. Millionaire, I would have nothing more pressing in life than to become poor again in order to have the right to drink good wine and eat delicious fowl. The finest things in life are meant for the poor, exclusively, and rich people have the right only to garbage and tortures. You will understand later, I hope. Now I have said my piece. Take your hat and get the hell out of here!"

Wealth has such a power to degrade and cretinize that it would be the most surprising miracle if such words had made any impression at all. One can imagine for himself the soul of a rich man under the layers of darkness, in a gulf comparable to the bottom of the deepest sea. It is absolute night, unimaginable silence, infinity, the habitacle of the monsters of silence. All the thunder and all the cannons on earth can burst and rumble at the surface of it. The soul, squatting in that abyss, is none the wiser. Even in the most obscure subterranean places, one can suppose that there are pale threads of light, one knows not whence they come, floating in the air like the *Virgin's threads* [of light] in the countryside, in the summertime. The catacombs, they too, are not immensely silent. There is, to the attentive ear, something that could be very distant pulsations coming from the center of the earth. But the Ocean does not forgive. Light, noise, movement, imperceptible vibrations – it gobbles up everything, forever.

# Chapter 16: The Sweating System

*"I have always been struck by the venerable bearing of old convicts."* – JULES VALLÈS.

*"In '93, there was, in Meudon, a tannery of human hides. The hides of women were practically good for nothing, being of too tender a fabric."*
– MONTGAILLARD.

An ancient poem from the Middle Ages, *Yvain ou le Chavalier au Lion*, shows that even in that pious century of Saint Bernard, Louis VII, and Philippe-Auguste, the industrial exploitation that consists in making gold from the flesh and blood of women already existed.

That chevalier Yvain, whom a friendly lion accompanies, arrives before the chateau of the *Worst Adventure*: "Hey! poor devil, where are you off to?" cried the people of the burg that he traverses on his way up to the keep. He does not listen to them, he pushes aside the porter who wants to stop him, and he enters into that vast hall giving onto an inner courtyard closed off by a palisade of sharp pikes. Let us translate the old language of Chrestien de Troyes:

> *Through the pikes, he saw there as many as three hundred virgins occupied at divers labors of silk and gold. They all did better than they knew. But such was their poverty that many among them, the poor, wore dresses*

*undone and untied, and their corsages
with holes worn in them at their
breasts and elbows, and they wore
dirty chemises on their backs. For
hunger and misease, their necks were
slender, their visages pale. Yvain sees
them and they see him. All lower their
head and weep, and they stay there a
long moment not knowing what will
happen. They cannot lift their eyes off
the ground, they are so discouraged.*

Yvain retraced his steps and interrogated the chateau's porter:

*"By your father's soul, tell me, who
are those demoiselles that I saw in the
courtyard, weaving silken fabrics and
orfrays? Their handiwork appears
very beautiful, but what does not seem
beautiful to me is that they are, in
body and visage, thin and pale, and
doleful. Nonetheless they would be, I
believe, beautiful and pleasant to behold if only they had something that
gave them pleasure."*

*"I will not tell you, no," responded the
porter, "find someone else to tell
you."*

Yvain then goes looking for someone to tell him and ends up finding the door of the courtyard where the demoiselles are working, and he draws near and greets them all together, and he notices the tears that fall from their eyes down their faces.

Yvain interrogates them in turn, and one of them makes him understand that they are captives of the devil's sons and that they cannot be delivered save by a good chevalier who "will kill the devil's sons in battle." But why deceive oneself with such vain hope?

> *"Nevermore will we have anything that pleases us. I have just said a very silly thing when I spoke of deliverance. Never will we leave here. Always will we be weaving silk fabrics and we will never be any better dressed. Always will we be poor and always will we be hungry and thirsty. No matter how much we gain, that will not make us eat any better. It is with great difficulty that we get some bread, a little in the morning and less in the evening. As for what we gain, each of us conserves for her upkeep merely four deniers on the pound and that is not enough to have sufficiency of clothes or nourishment... However, there is not a single one of us whose work does not bring in twenty sous or more a week. A duke would be rich therefrom and we are in great poverty, and he for whom we labor is rich by our own merit. To make ends meet, we work well into the wee hours of the night, and entire days. If we want to*

*repose one instant, we are menaced
with torture to our limbs. That is why
we do dare not take any repose."*[46]

After eight centuries, the same evil is horrify-
ingly aggravated. The poor captives delivered by the
good chevalier Yvain – for he delivered them, if one
is to believe his trouvère – were three hundred in
number. Now listen to Leo Tolstoy:

*"In front of the house where I live
there is a factory of silk preparation
adhering to the latest instructions in
technique. Three thousand women and
seven hundred men live and work
there. From my house, I hear the in-
cessant noise of their machines, and I
know, for I have gone over there, what
it means. Three thousand women,
standing for twelve hours, are in front
of their workbenches and surrounded
by a terrible noise, they wind and un-
wind the silk threads with which they
make fabrics. All those women, with
the exception of those who have ar-
rived recently from the countryside,
have a sickly look to them. The majority of them lead a depraved and im-
moral life. Almost all, married or not,
immediately after giving birth, send
their children into the countryside or*

---

[46]Original footnote: Citation taken from an excellent article:
*Femmes esclaves*, signed R. Périé, in the "Pages libres" Review,
issue 3 August 1901.

*to a nursery where 90 percent of them die, and their mothers, so as not to be replaced, come back to the factory, two or three days after giving birth. Thus, for twenty years, I know that tens of thousands of young and strong mothers have died; and that, now also, mothers continue to destroy their life and that of their children in order to prepare velour or silk fabric.*"[47]

The good Tolstoy is overwhelmed. But what is the factory he is talking about compared to the immense *sweathouses* in America or England? In France alone there are more than six million women factory workers out of less than twenty million women in all. More powerful statistic than a Shakespearean tragedy. That apocalyptic multitude of famished creatures working, suffering, dying, so as to ensure the delight of a few; without light to work in, without light to suffer, without light to die by, and that for generations and throughout the centuries!

Outside the factories, the same statistic speaks of a barbarous army, a famished horde of 250,000 male and female workers living, or trying to live, in Paris alone, on work at home; while the work of the Hebrews in Egypt represent, for the people who exploit them, profits that are able to go from a thousand to eighteen hundred percent.[48]

---

[47]Original footnote: Tolstoy, *The Rays of Dawn*.

[48]Original footnote: This book, not being a work of documentation, a single example will be enough to exempt me from an infinity of others. M. Georges Mény, in his book: *Le Travail a bon*

Try as one may to multiply these usurious numbers, already diabolical, one will arrive, if that is even possible, at an almost exact proportion of wealth to poverty. Do one hundred thousand poor people suffice to make one single rich person? It is a question for the West. In Asia, in the colossal swarming of China or India, a million is needed perhaps.

*The Sweating System!* One has difficulty understanding how these impious words could have been written, even in English, which is, however, the language of injustice, of infernal harshness, the language of the least generous of all peoples. Yes, even in English, it is not to be believed. But the sweat of what? My God! It is impossible, after hearing such a word, not to think on Gethsemane, not to think on Moses who wanted all Egypt to flow with blood so as to prefigure the Agony of the Son of God. He who as-

---

*marché,* has established as follows the cost price of a dozen women's hats sold at 4 fr. 80 a piece:

| | |
|---|---|
| Worker's salary for the dozen..... | 2 fr. 40 |
| Contractor's wage........................ | 0 fr. 80 |
| Forms........................................... | 3 fr. 00 |
| Trimming...................................... | 4 fr. 75 |
| Flowers........................................ | 3 fr. 45 |
| Total: | 14 fr. 40 |

Those twelve hats will be sold altogether for 57 f. 60. The firm that launches them and the department stores that sell them will earn therefore a total 43 fr. 20, while each woman worker will have earned 2 fr. 40!!!

sumed all imaginable, and all unimaginable, suffering, has he sweated blood then in that fashion? The Sweating of Blood *systematically*. The Sweating of Jesus' Blood calculated to finance famines or massacres!... One may suppose that men have gone crazy to have gone and leaned over that chasm...

What is even more incomprehensible in the world is the patience of the poor, somber and *miraculous* medal of God's Patience in his palaces of light. When suffering has been too remote, it would seem however quite simple to beat the daylights out of, or gut, the ferocious beast. There are examples of that. They are even plentiful in History. But, always, these revolts were convulsive movements and of short duration. Immediately after the outburst, the Sweating of Jesus' Blood begins again silently, at night, under the tranquil olive trees in the Garden, the disciples ever sleeping. He must continue that Agony for so many miserable wretches – for a very great number of defenseless beings – men, women, and children above all!

For here is the horror of horrors: the labor of children, the misery of all the little ones exploited by industry in the production of riches! And that in every land. Jesus said: "Let the children come to me."[49] The rich people say: "Send them to the factory, to the workshop, into the darkest and most mortal places of our hells. The efforts of their feeble arms will add something to our opulence."

One sees those poor children, that a man's

---

[49]Let the children come to me: Matthew 19:14.

breath could blow over, furnish a labor of more than thirty hours a week, and those workers, O vengeful God! can be counted in the hundreds of thousands. So that no one may say that religion has been forgotten, the little girls' workshops, unknown to Dante, are often directed by nuns, consecrated virgins, as dry as the Devil's kindling, and who know just the right trick for ensuring maximum output...

Perhaps the high-society girl does not know, she neither – like Dante – what her toilette and her fine furbelows cost. Why would anyone mention to her the mortal fatigue, the never-satisfied hunger of the little wretches, only too flattered to knock themselves out for her beauty? Who would want to try to make that pretty brute understand the bitterness of devoured tears and the perpetual constriction of those little hearts? But, because those *bagatelles* are infinitely greater than her, and because there is, all the same, a justice, one can be certain that she will not be ignorant of them forever. And then...!

The evangelist Saint Luke heard the Sweat of Jesus Christ's Blood falling on the ground, drop by drop. That so faint sound, incapable of waking the disciples who were asleep, must have been heard by the most distant constellations and it singularly modified their trajectory. What to think of the sound, feebler still and much less audible, of the innumerable footsteps of those poor children going to their task of suffering and misery demanded by the accursed, but, all the same, without knowing it and without anyone else knowing it, going in that way to their great brother in the Garden of Agony who calls to them and waits for them with his bleeding outstretched arms. *Sinite pueros venire ad me. Talium est enim regnum Dei.*[50]

---

[50]*Sinite... Dei*: Matthew 19:14.

# Chapter 17: Commerce

*"Am I my brother's keeper?"* – CAIN.

Formerly, quite a long time ago, when there the nobility and crusading knights still existed, commerce *caused a loss in rank and title*. It was an absolute law, a fundamental law. A gentleman who engaged in commerce was, by that very act, discredited, disqualified, fallen, demonetized, dishonored, eradicated from the soil, roots up in the air. And it was perfectly just and reasonable. Even today when arithmetic has replaced nobility, commerce still retains something of its ancient stink, and one does not avow it very voluntarily.

Why then is it so despicable? It is because it devours the poor, because it is a war waged on the poor, simply. Retailers of all sorts: bakers, butchers, pork butchers, coal men, landlords, etc. make their profit really on the poor, who are always incapable of stocking up for the future or benefiting from opportunities. *Half of five is three*, that is the arithmetic of retailers. Here is some bread at 0 fr. 35 cent. a kilo. The poor person who cannot buy anything other than a pound at a time will pay four *sous*. If he is hungry two times a day, at the end of the month the baker will have stolen 1 fr. 50 from him. And so with the others. A filthy room is rented for eight francs a week, more than four hundred francs a year, to a poverty-stricken woman who knocks herself out earning two francs a day.

Credit is a fat calf of old – butchered to celebrate the return of the Prodigal Son reintegrating into the paternal six-story mansion after having herded swine for the longest time. Tell a merchant: "I cannot accept that anyone doubts the probity of a man whom one does not know." He will never understand. In the language of that ignoble man, *to know* someone means to know that he has money and not to know him means not to know whether he has money. A known man is a rich man. Catastrophe of the Word fallen into the mud. In the first case, overzealous esteem, the lowest servility; in the second, defiance and hostility. It is impure and unclean, but commercial in all senses of the word.

The exclusive desire to enrich oneself is, without contradiction, the most abject act imaginable. Supposing that it were possible to really compare, that is to say in the Absolute, an artist and a merchant, it would be an experience to make the earth come unhinged.

Instinctively, without his having any need to know it, the former tends toward Suffering, Poverty, complete Despoilment, because there are no other abysses and because his attraction is to the bottom of the abyss. The latter amasses, believing that he knows what he does. He amasses like an insect and prepares and conditions for himself a small tomb with the straw of others' famine and the detritus of their misery. It is what he calls *making a fortune*. On the one hand, a man searching for Beauty, Light, liberating Splendor; on the other, a slave constraining his soul to rummage through the garbage!

"One cannot do anything without money," is a

commonplace, the sacrilegious stupidity of which is perfectly ignored by those who employ it. Without a doubt, nothing can be done without the sweat and blood of the poor; but that sweat, when it flows from a noble brow, and that blood, when it streams forth from a generous heart – it is not for the dogs to come and lap it up, and it is a horror to witness it.

Fundamentally, commerce consists in selling very dearly what one bought very cheaply, while deceiving as much as possible on the quantity and the quality. In other words, commerce takes the drop of Blood from the Savior given gratuitously to each man and makes that drop more precious than entire worlds, dreadfully multiplied by the additions or admixtures, a more or less remunerative traffic.

"I do not force you to come and visit me," says the usurer who is behind every merchant. "Of course, dog, you do not force me; but necessity does, invincible necessity, and you know that very well."

Viewed from on high, commerce is a veritable sacrilege. The Jews, eldest Race compared to whom all other nations are children, and who have had, consequently, the ability to go much further towards evil than other men towards good, the profound Jews must feel that this is so. They are the fathers of commerce just as they were the fathers of that Son of Man, their own purest Blood, whom it was necessary, by divine decree, that they should purchase and sell one certain day. Their nearest neighbors of extraction, the Carthaginians of Carthage, lost ancestors of the Carthaginians of England, must have been their good students. That is certainly not said to diminish them.

When they are converted, as has been foretold, their commercial prowess will be converted as well. Instead of selling dear what will have cost them little, they will give by the handsful what will have cost them everything. Their thirty deniers, soaked in the Savior's Blood, will become something like thirty centuries of humility and hope, and that will be unimaginably beautiful.

To fall from there into modern trade is to make one feel afraid, it is to make one feel disgusted with life and death. One has spoken at length about the Jewish abjection. It is a question now, of course, of trafficking Jews, of the Jewish dregs, exception made for very noble individuals who have maintained a proud heart, a "truly Israelite"[51] heart under the terrible *Velamen* of Saint Paul. In what way will that so famous abjection surpass the servility of the haughtiest shopkeeper vis-à-vis a client presumed rich and his boorish insolence with respect to another client supposed poor? If one wants that their ignoble attitudes should be equal in appearance, there will always be, even at that level, the immense birthright of the chosen Race and the enormous preeminence of twenty centuries of very carefully recorded humiliations. The Jewish abjection can invoke lightning, the commercial abjection of Christians can attract merely showers of spit and dejections.

Does anyone wonder how a merchant spends his hours of leisure? Horror of a poor soul! Not reading, not a single generous thought, not a consoling

---

[51]Original footnote: "*Ecce vere Israelita, in quo dolus non est.*" The Gospel according to Saint John.

memory, no other hope than to continue on the morrow the previous days' turpitudes. The money gained, stolen, the dance of figures, and the pit of the tomb. The very poor people whom he fleeces experience delights that he has no idea of. Even those who have lost everything, except their tears, can be consoled by a book, by a word of kindness, by caressing a miserable beast, by the sight of a humble dead child's plaything, by whatever object of no value able to evoke a memory of grief or joy, by no means costing a thing, not worth anything, unable to tempt anyone, and kept religiously like a treasure, to the very end. It is for those people doubtless that Jesus wept over Lazarus' tomb. "I bless you, O Father, Lord in heaven as on earth, for having hidden these things from the wise and prudent and for having revealed them to the little people."

"Business is business," another diabolical commonplace. A merchant capable of pity apart from his trade – something of the sort has been seen before, it appears – becomes immediately merciless when his commercial interests are at stake, even when the smallest profit is involved, most disdained by him – because at that instant the priest or the pontiff of Mammon appears. But if he is in the Jupiterian position of a creditor, he shows himself to be terrible, precisely because the debt represents nothing to him – only because he believes it to be a matter of Justice. The Justice of Cain, saying that he "is not his brother's keeper" and believing maybe to justify himself in this way for having assassinated him. He is horribly mistaken, adding to his fratricide a more inexpiable fratricide.

"Whether you like it or not, Mr. Grocer, you are the keeper of all your brothers, and if your dirty house crumbles from that *fraternity* there, so much the better! You will gain *equality*, with those who suffer, and *liberty* for your soul." It is the only tolerable application of the republican motto that cretinizes us and has been poisoning us for one hundred years now.

# Chapter 18: The Solicitor of the Holy Sepulcher

*"L'histoire des Juifs barre l'histoire du genre humain, comme un digue barre un fleuve, pour en élever le niveau."[52]* – LÉON BLOY.

*This Chapter is dedicated by the author of* Salvation Through the Jews *to his friend Raoul Simon.*

Yes! [The Solicitor] of the Holy Sepulcher! and it has to do with a Jew, a Jewish poet, a totally extraordinary man who has never been converted. But he was a Jew profoundly and, by consequence, the greatest poet the Poor ever had, which places him very near to the Tomb of Jesus Christ, infinitely nearer than the majority of Christians.

One knows that Godfrey de Bouillon did not accept being King of Jerusalem, but only the *Solicitor* or Defender of the Holy Sepulcher, "not wanting," so say the *Assises*,[53] "to wear a crown of gold there where the King of kings wore a crown of thorns." There can be no question of royalty or a golden crown for the poet Morris Rosenfeld, but never have the poor had such a defender. The Holy City of his fathers, which he conquered, it is poetry itself, which is

---

[52]*L'histoire... niveau*: French for "The history of the Jews dams up the history of human kind like a dike that dams up a river, in order to raise the water level." Chapter VIII in *Salvation Through the Jews*, Léon Bloy, Sunny Lou Publishing, 2020.

[53]*Assises*: in this case, the rules, laws, statutes, &c. of a kingdom as determined by an assembly of peers.

the Jerusalem of the poor and sorrowful.

Poet of the poverty-stricken, poverty-stricken himself, and expressing himself in a poverty-stricken language. "Ruined and exhausted by long exile, chased and dispersed in a foreign land, we have lost our sacred language and our dignity of former days, and, today, we must content ourselves with the sighs exhaled in a poor and ridiculed dialect that we have appropriated during the period that we pulled along among the people living there." But poets do what poets want. That cosmopolite jargon formed of the rags of all languages, he made a music of it for lamentable harps.

Morris (Moses-Jacob) Rosenfeld was born in Russian Poland. There, at the edge of a river both calm and furious, his father, a very poor fisherman, recounted to him stories of revolts and sufferings in order to make his heart grow. "We have not always been a people capable only of weeping..." Called on to continue in the footsteps of all the sufferers and to be poorer still than his fathers had been, he was consoled all his life by the memory of his humble childhood passed in the neighborhood of the river, hills, and forests.

> *The sun goes down behind the mountains.... The water flows, always flows and murmurs a language that nobody understands. A solitary barque sails in the distance, without a boatman, without a rudder; one could say that the devils push it forward. In that barque an infant cries... Long golden rings*

> *fall onto his shoulders, and the poor*
> *little man looks on while sighing...*
> *And the barque continues to sail.*
> *While waving in the air with his all-*
> *white handkerchief, he salutes me*
> *from afar, the poor little man bids me*
> *adieu, charming child. And my heart*
> *begins to grow agitated. One might*
> *say that something weeps... Tell me,*
> *what is going on then? Oh! that su-*
> *perb little man, I know who he is. My*
> *God! it is my childhood that vanishes!*

Limpid source that soon will become a torrent of bitter tears. The poor man, however, is not a rebel. His nature does not bring him to cry vengeance: True Jewish lamenter, he knows only how to weep over his unfortunate brothers even more than over himself. But his tears have a force of invocation more fearful than torrents of despair. I really do not know if there exists in poetry anything more agonizing than the piece entitled, *To a Cloud*:

> *Stop there, wild cloud, stop.*
> *And tell me whence you come and whither you go.*
> *Why are you so somber, so heavy, and so dark?*
> *I am afraid of you, you frighten my soul.*
> . . . . . . . . . . . . . . . . . . . . . . . . . . .
> *Tell me: is it the horrible wind of Black Russia*
> *That chases you here?*
> . . . . . . . . . . . . . .
> *Perhaps you carry within you*
> *Old patience, which soon*
> *Will explode, bloody and savage.*

. . . . . . . . . . . . . . . . . . . . . . . . . . . .

*But, as my head was lifted towards the sky,*
*Suddenly a drop fell from the cloud;*
*A bitter drop fell into my mouth –*
*Bitter, more bitter than bile.*
*And it seems to me, brothers – I am sure of it,*
*Oh! yes, yes, that is a Jewish tear of blood.*
*A Jewish tear – how horrible it is!*
*It tears my soul out, and I lose my head.*
*A Jewish tear, my God! I am losing myself –*
*But it is a blend of gall, brain, and blood,*
*A Jewish tear! – I recognized it at once.*
*It smells of persecution, adversity, and* pogrom.[54]
*The Jewish tear, oh! I smell in its odor*
*The dreadful blasphemy of two thousand years...*
*The Jewish tear... Now I understand*
*What sort of cloud it was.*

That crushed man at the bottom of crypts seems to have sensed, more than any other man, the frightening and supernatural sadness of that Holy Week which lasts two thousand years for him and that is all the history of the Jews after the Vendition of the First Born. But also, more than another, he sensed its beauty. Some of his poems are like echoes in the sepulcher of the grandiose Liturgy of the *Tenebrae* drawn entirely from the divine Book that the Jews carry with them over the face of the earth, while trying to read it through the somber tissue of their *Velamen*:

*An old and torn book. The cover full of*

---

[54]Original footnote: Massacre of Jews.

*blood and tears. Do you know that*
*book? Without a doubt you now know*
*it, that book, I'm sure of it. The most*
*holy of holy books. We have already*
*given much for that poor book...*

And that sublime cry at the sight of emigrant
Jews and their lamentable bundles on the quays of
New York:

*With them, in those sacks – do you see? –*
*Are found the world's treasure – their Torah! –*
*How can one say that such a nation is poor?*
*A people who traverses thru the night & tombs;*
*Who knows how to pass thru horror, fire, death,*
*To save what is holy and dear to it?*
*Who knows how to resist so many misfortunes;*
*Who knows too well how to suffer & shed blood;*
*Who fears nothing & fears nobody;*
*Who risks its life for poor pieces of paper?*
*A people who always bathes in tears:*
*Whom everyone strikes & finds joy in torturing;*
*Who wanders for millennia in the deserts,*
*And has not yet lost courage?*
*To pronounce the name of a such a people,*
*You must dry your lips.*
*– On your knees, before it, O nations!*

The man who speaks like that is, in the eyes of
the world, a little less than a worm. But he is infinitely right, and God himself could not say it better. The
Jews are the firstborn of everyone, and when things
are in their places, their proudest masters will consider themselves honored to lick their vagabond feet. Be-

cause everything is promised to them, and, while waiting, they do penitence for the world. The right of the firstborn cannot be annulled by a punishment, however rigorous it might be, and God's word of honor is unmodifiable, because "his gifts and his vocation are without repentance." It is the greatest among converted Jews who said so, and implacable Christians who claim to eternalize the reprisals of the *Crucifigatur* ought to remember it. "Their crime," said Saint Paul again, "was the salvation of nations." What an extraordinary people is that then, of whom God asks permission to save the human race, after having assumed its flesh the better to suffer? Is that to say that his Passion would not have contented Him, if it had not been inflicted on Him by his beloved people, and that any other blood than what He had from Abraham would have been inefficacious to wash away the sins of the world?

Assuredly Rosenfeld, who was merely an extremely ignorant laborer, must not have read Saint Paul whom the Jews scarcely read. But his genius as a poet and his profound sense of Race made him see these things well enough. As soon as he began to sing, his place was – I said it at the beginning – on the right of the Tomb of Jesus Christ. Without knowing it, he continued the imperishable Affirmations of the Apostle of nations and, having been a poet only and ever for the poor, he found himself – in the most mysterious sense – the Solicitor of the Holy Sepulcher, king without a crown and without the robe of poetry of those who weep, lost sentinel of the Tomb of the God of the Poor happily immolated by his ancestors. Then, by the power alone of venerable laws, his Judaism was exceeded, outflanked on all sides by the feeling of a universal confraternity with the poor and the suffering peoples o'er all the earth.

His perpetual, truly Hebrew, vagabondage, predisposed him to it. Under the reign of Alexander III and his minister Ignatief, the situation of the Jews in Russia was no longer tenable. Outraged, chased, massacred, the savage empire had become a hell to them. Rosenfeld took up the walking stick of a wandering life and departed.

"For four years," one of his admirers[55] said, "he was chased by the winds from one place to another; for four years, each wave of misery swallowed him up and spit him out, leaving him at the mercy of another wave; for four years he was shaken by a sort of fever that existed only among the Jewish people – *the search for a home*. That pitiless fever, for twenty centuries, leaves no time to rest to the children of Israel; that life of a vagabond dog, without rights and without esteem, without country and without hope, merchant, always a merchant, from Orient to Occident, from North to Midi, crossing the mountains and traversing the Oceans, praying and crying, weeping and fighting, that ignoble and iniquitous life, one can say that our poet knew it well."

In his ode *"Sur le sein de l'Ocean,"*[56] two Jews, whose entrance into America is denied, return to Europe:

---

[55]Original footnote: FAINSILBER-RUSU. Speaking to a group of Zionist students at a conference in Montpellier, June 1906.

[56]*Sur... Ocean*: French for "On the Ocean's Bosom."

*Who are you, poor wretch, tell me,*
*You who impose silence on the most terrible*
                                                          *[distress,*
*You who have neither sobs nor tears*
*At the very gates of horrible Death?*
. . . . . . . . . . . . . . . . . . . . . . . . . . . .
*We had a lodging, but it was destroyed,*
*They burned what was most sacred to us;*
*They made bone heaps of our dearest & best.*
*Others were led away, hands bound.*
. . . . . . . . . . . . . . . . . . . . . . . . . . . .
*We are the Jews, the disinherited Jews,*
*Friendless & joyless, without hope for happiness.*
. . . . . . . . . . . . . . . . . . . . . . . . . . . .
*We are miserable like stones.*
*The ungrateful earth refuses to accord us a place.*
. . . . . . . . . . . . . . . . . . . . . . . . . . . .
*Let it boil, froth, and redden in the abyss:*
*Whatever happens, we are the abandoned Jews.*

If the Jews are worthy of a such a poet, they
will pardon him for having often wept over others as
well. Over and beyond the colossal misfortune of the
ancient people of Jehovah, Rosenfeld's universal soul
perceived other misfortunes and did not hide his having a broken heart. He had been so well placed to recognize them! He had seen them working among the
poorest workers of all nations, in Amsterdam, in London, in New York where, for ten years, he had no other means of existence than the sad profession of a factory worker-tailor. His verses on the despicable slav-
ery of the factories are perhaps the most sorrowful.

Dazed after a day's work, the worker returns

home. His wife and child are waiting for him:

*Work chases me early from the home,*
*And does not let me return until late.*
*Alas! my flesh is a stranger to me!*
*The look of my child is that of a stranger!*

His wife speaks to him about their child. The child is clever and all day long asks about nothing but his father. But now he sleeps. The poor man approaches the child's cradle. He holds out to him a small coin and speaks to him in order to wake him up, to show it to him.

*A dream agitates his lips.*
*– Oh! where is he then, where is papa?*
*I'm right here, full of distress, grief*
*And bitterness, and I think:*
*When you awaken at daylight, child,*
*I will no longer be here.*

One day finally the poet, having drawn attention to himself, quit the factory, and unknown protectors offered him the worst profession of journalism, which soon becomes almost intolerable for him: "Oh! open the doors of the workshop. I will endure anything. – Suck my blood, factory, oh! suck my blood! I will cry only partially. I will do my heavy burden. I will do it without protest. – I can praise my scissors. But my quill must not belong to anyone but me."

His quill! Is that really the right word? At every moment the tailor Rosenfeld makes me think of those tailors in images from so long ago, of those barbarian, puerile, and sublime artists, who knew nothing of any science or any art, not having received lessons from any other master than their suffering, and working as best they can with poor instruments, under the high windows of a compassionate workshop.

When he sings the suffering of the wandering People, the hellish torments of the homicidal factory, and the so dolorous lament of the poor seduced girl: "Do you remember the evening when you dishonored me?" or the eternal beauty of a kind and terrible nature – I always see him sculpting, with fatigue, a piece of very hard wood which is not perhaps what would be needed, by means of one does not know what humble knife that he sharpens, twenty times a day, on the indestructible millstone of pitiless hearts. It does not always go according to plan. That wood is like iron and his tool chips sometimes on some invincible and unexpected knot that deranges his composition. Then the naïve artist, deprived of method, does not always know how to employ it on such and such an image already begun. So the knife grinds furiously and the difficulty becomes for him an occasion of discoveries that make one shiver.

However uneven his work might be, someone summed Rosenfeld up perfectly when he called him *the poet of proletarians*. He is that more than anyone, because he is Jewish and because the Jews are essentially proletarian. But the proletarian – like the tears – of all peoples and all times. Only, Jewish tears are the heaviest. They have the weight of many centuries. Those of the poet have been generously shed on a great number of unfortunate people who were not of his same Race, and now you can see them, those precious tears, in the balance of the Judge of human sorrows who does not make a distinction between peoples and persons.

When the Father wants the Firstborn to assume his place again, I imagine the most splendid night lighting up the feast, the moon's gentle crescent marking the place of the Holy Sepulcher, and the tears of all the poor glimmering indistinctly, unimaginably, from the furthest reaches of heaven!

# Chapter 19: Two Cemeteries

*"The constellation of the Little Dog, is it not in the austral hemisphere?"*

The first is barely worth talking about. It is that of the poor, the common pit, the cartage of the *Maccabees*,[57] the scramble, the blasphemy, and the filth of dirty undertakers who have no hope for any gratuity. When deaths abound, it is the rapid clearing away and profaning of the provisorily interred whose bones no longer have the right to a semblance of a sepulcher and which are thrown into a pile, like rubble or impurities into some hole.

Sometimes, to tell the truth, it is the Crematorium which Christians might believe to be exclusively reserved only for atheists, whose formal will it is to be burned after their death. Error that must be stopped. The Administration does not frown on warming its furnace for the *mutilated* remains of indigents that are assassinated in hospitals and that no parent claims. They must be gotten rid of, and we are no longer living in barbarous times when brotherhoods existed for the burial and charitable sepulture

---

[57]Cartage of the *Maccabees*: a reference to the uprising and revolt of the Maccabees. But also possibly in particular reference, as Bloy references it elsewhere in his writings, to the Holy Maccabean Martyrs: a woman and her seven sons, along with a teacher of theirs, arrested altogether and massacred, one by one, by Antiochus IV Epiphanes, the Seleucid King, who tried to force them to eat pork, which they refused, it being against their religion. The story is told in 2 Maccabees.

of the abandoned.

But let us get back to the so-called *Parisian* cemetery, *extra-muros*, necropolis of the poor who multiply around Paris: Bagneux, Pantin, Ivry, etc., for the dead are loathed just like the living. Sodom does not want them, and they are carted as far off as possible. There is at least for these slumberers the benefit of solitude. In the spring or autumn, when one is very miserable, these distant places can, all the same, appear lovely.

The Administration which has condemned the ancient use of the monumental Cross at the moment even when it multiplied the *sign* of it derisively in the systematic layout of suburban cemeteries, has consented to plant, along the avenues, a rather large number of trees. At the commencement, that geometric and verdure-less plane would cause despair. Now that the trees have grown tall, and have been able to plunge their roots into the hearts of the deceased, they let fall, with their melancholic shadows, a grave gentleness...

Let us go stroll among the tombs. Many are uncultivated, abandoned completely, arid like cinders. They are those of the awfully poor who have not got a friend left among the living and whom nobody remembers. They were shoved in there, one certain day, because they needed to be put somewhere. A son or a brother, sometimes an ancestor, has come up with the money for a cross, then the three or four conveyors have something to drink, and after several drunken sentences they go their separate ways. And it is all over. The hole is filled in, the gravedigger has planted the cross with blows of a pick and has gone off to have a drink himself. No fencing has ever been, nor ever will be, installed by anyone to mark the place where that poor person rests, who is perhaps at the right hand of Jesus Christ... Under the weight of rains, the earth has sunken in, and the stones have gone off in such great numbers that even the thistles cannot survive there. Soon the cross will fall over, rot on the soil, the name of the poor wretch will be effaced and no longer exist save in the registers of the dead...

What tugs at the heartstrings is the throng of small tombs. One needs to see that spectacle to know just how many children are killed in the abattoirs of misery. Entire rows almost of small white cradles can be seen there, surmounted by absurd crowns made of glass pearls and medallions bought at the bazaar where execrable sentimentalities are put on display. There are however some naïve ones. Here and there, in a sort of niche fixed to the cross, are exposed, with photography of the dead child, humble playthings that amused him for a few days. Sometimes a desolate, old woman is on her knees in front of one of them. She is so old that she cannot even cry anymore. But her lamentation is so grievous that strangers cry for her...[58]

After the cemetery for the poor, it is an even more bizarre feeling to visit the Dog Cemetery. Many people probably do not know that it exists. It goes without saying that it is the cemetery for rich dogs, poor dogs having no place there.

---

[58]Original footnote: LÉON BLOY. *La Femme pauvre*.

A certain effort is needed to get used to the thought of a necropolis of dogs. It exists however, in Asnières, on a small island, charming otherwise, in the Seine. Yes, the dogs have their own cemetery, a real and beautiful cemetery with plots from three to thirty years, a provisional vault, more or less sumptuous monuments, and even a *common grave* for economical idolaters first of all, but above all, one supposes, so that poor people, belonging to the human race, might feel less insulted.

Article 5 of the rule book is admirable: "All religious emblems and all monuments affecting the form of human sepulchers are strictly prohibited in the *zoological* cemetery." The public has been warned, by that last word, that the founder, male or female, is a knowledgeable person who does not speak in vain. We are not dogs ourselves nor sentimental imbeciles, but zoologists, thinkers. And that sheds a singular light on the prohibition, so very little Jesuitic, of religious emblems. It would seem, in fact, that that prohibition is in view of preventing profanations, but it suffices to cast a glance at the monuments to assure oneself of a voluntary and solidly corseted atheism. For example:

*If Your Soul*, O Sappho, *does not accompany mine,*
*O dear and noble Friend, on unknown sojourns,*
I do not want Heaven! *I want, whatever happens,*
*To sleep by Your side, without waking, forever.*

These verses, heroically constructed, by an old millionairess blue-stocking on the rotting carcass of her beloved dog, say enough and maybe even a little too much. But the zoology saves everything. Their only concern is that visitors should believe themselves to be in a garden. As for "the form *strictly* prohibited to human sepulchers," the most one can say is that that clause is a nice little joke. A myope, incapable of deciphering the inscriptions on the tombs and non the wiser, will necessarily think that he is in a cemetery, pagan assuredly and very bizarre, but human, and he does not see anything that disabuses him of that impression. There are grotesque and costly monuments, the ridiculousness of which is nothing excessive nor humiliating for the best of company and which would be perfectly suitable for the carcasses of the most distinguished gentlemen. The epitaphs, it must be confessed, leave no doubt, but only the epitaphs.

The monotony of "eternal regrets" is a bit tiring. The formula of loyalty, more canine than the dogs themselves: "I will weep for you forever, and I will never replace you" superabounds plentifully. Nevertheless the patient visitor is recompensed.

"My Ponnette, protect forever your mistress." – "Kiki, too good to live." – "Drack, he loved us too much and could not live." – "Linda, dead for attachment, loyalty, intelligence, and *originality*." – (Two niches below.) "The destiny that unites them on earth reunites them in death." – (Beneath a military tent.) "Produced by a collection of artillerymen." – "Over your body the spring will scatter rose petals." – "She was our entire life." – "To Folette, O my so beloved darling/You were the smile in my life./What epitaph could tell/How much my heart will have wept for you?" – "The brutality of men has put an end to our love." – And this one, oh! this one: "Mimiss, her gramma to her *trouneniouniousse*!"

I cannot more highly recommend a glorious monument attributable perhaps to Desaix or Kléber, and I do not know what colossal capital, at the center of which is seen an enormous heart in *ex-voto* blazoned with the name of a dog in golden letters. There are also coronets of marquis, counts, viscounts, a torsade, and even a crown firmly placed on the cross, which is prohibited however. But princes are refused nothing and one is in the aristocratic rottenness of dogs, at several million leagues from proletarians.

One has to wonder whether their stupidity is not more detestable than their nastiness even. I do not think that contempt for the poor has ever been more clearly, more insolently, declared. Is it the effect of a demonic idolatry or of a transcendent imbecility? There are monuments there that have cost the subsistence of twenty families! I have seen, in winter, on some of the animals' graves, sprays of flowers whose price would have satisfied the hunger of fifty poor people for an entire day! And those eternal regrets, those lyrical expressions of emotion by the bastards and bitches who would not give a cent to one of their brothers dying of hunger! "The more I see men, the more I love my dog," said the monument to Jappy, miserable mongrel cur whose ignoble marble effigy cries vengeance to heaven. The greater part of those niches, lacking barking sounds, are adorned, for the consolation of the survivors, with a photograph of the rotting animal. Almost all are hideous, in probable conformity with the stinking souls of their masters or mistresses. "Attractions," said Fourier, "are proportional to those destined to receive them."[59]

I have not had the joy of attending a first-class interment. What a lost opportunity. The long mourning veils, the flower bushes, the clamors and sobs of despair, the discourses perhaps. Unfortunately, there is not a chapel. With a little music, Beethoven's *Funeral March*, for example, it would have been easy for me to evoke the memory of the lamentable creatures in the image of God, carried, after their death, into the mass graves of Public Assistance and buried with the boot kicks of drunkards.

"Every wooden box carrying a dead animal," says article 9 of the Rule book, "will be opened for *verification*, upon entry into the cemetery." That very sage article has clearly anticipated the case where some extremely rich whore wanted to have her father buried there.

---

[59]Attractions... them: Which would seem to suggest that the owners tend to choose dogs that look like them. Or it could mean simply that beauty is in the eye of the beholder. Or both.

# Conclusion

*"Iota unum."*[60] – The Gospel according to MATTHEW.

"Your book," a poor wretch told me, "has nothing to do with reality."

I know. The evil of this world is of angelic origin and cannot be expressed in a human tongue. First the Disobedience, then the Fratricide. There you have it, the whole Story. But who knows the extent? Supposing even that an extraordinary man, a Moses or an Ezekiel, could have glimpsed the inconceivable prodigy of man's Freedom victorious over the divine Will, he would have lacked the wherewithal to recount that tragedy.

The one monster of Avarice disconcerts reason. The Apostle who was particularly invested in the instruction of nations said that avarice is Idolatry itself. The Holy Spirit that speaks through him left us on the edge of that chasm where no one can descend. Avarice which kills the poor is as inexplicable as Idolatry. Now idolatry is, as I have said before, a substitution of the Visible for the Invisible, something that is quite certainly the most monstrous, the most incomprehensible of attentats.

Without a doubt, the modern miser, landlord, merchant, or industrial magnate, does not worship sacks of *ecus* or wads of banknotes on a small altar in a small chapel. He does not kneel before those spoils of other men and does not address prayers or canticles

---

[60]*Iota unum*: Latin for "One jot." Matthew 5:18.

to them in the odoriferous smoke of a censer. But he proclaims that money is the only good, and he dedicates *all* his soul to it. Sincere cult, without hypocrisy, without lassitude, without renunciation. If he says, in the baseness of his heart and in his language, that he loves money for the delights that it procures him, he lies or he is horribly mistaken, that affirmation being a denial, at the very instant that he proffers it, by each of his acts, by the work and the immeasurable torments to which he condemns himself voluntarily for the acquisition or conservation of that money that is merely the visible figure of the Blood of Christ circulating in all his members.

Far from loving it for the material pleasures that he goes without, he worships it *in spirit and in truth*, just as the Saints worship God who made penitence a duty and martyrdom a glory for them. He worships it for those who do not worship it, he suffers in the stead of those who do not want to suffer for money. Misers are mystics! Everything they do is with a view to pleasing an invisible God whose visible simulacrum, so laboriously sought after, steeps them in tortures and ignominies.

The bill of exchange, and the promissory note, invented, it is said, by the Jews of the Middle Ages, but whose origin is much more ancient, given it goes back at least to the "chirograph" of Tobias, represents the double contrition of the miser who is disconsolate for being unable to pay it at term or for being forced, on paying it, to part with it. In the second case, that devotee forsakes God for God, tactical maneuver recommended by directors of conscience.

Yes, it is true, I have remained quite above my task. The evil procured by avarice is completely unspeakable, humanly irremediable. All that one can do is to aggravate the damnation of Cain by putting on his head the blood of his brother. And the only thing the rich man can do – if the demon should give him back his soul – is to renounce his riches. For it is indispensable that the Gospel be fulfilled and that the Kingdom of the Poor be constituted. That is the kingdom that is referred to, and no other, in the Dominical Orison: *Adveniat regnum tuum.*[61] "When you pray, pray like this," said the Lord. "Sell and give, renounce everything that you possess," strong and ineffaceable words that Christian cowardice, judging them too heroic, strives to strike sacrilegiously from the text by means of the ignoble and Jesuitic distinction between *precept* and *counsel,* which places the Gospel in the mud for three hundred years now.

It is often asked what the *Iota* in the Sermon on the Mount really refers to, the which *iota* must subsist and be fulfilled before heaven and earth can pass. A child could respond to that question. It is precisely the *Kingdom of the Poor*, the kingdom of the *voluntary* poor, by choice and by love. All else is vanity, lying, idolatry, and turpitude.

And now, let the renegades and imbeciles accuse me as much as they want of revolt or anarchy! I have foreseen and desired that incomparable honor of having against me all the bellies that are on high and all the hearts that are on low. For me, the most enormous tumults of hatred and anger will not drown out

---

[61]*Adveniat regnum tuum*: Thy kingdom come.

the appalling groaning, as witness the following:

*Heaven is not made for the poor folk like us.*

Unto death, I will remember having heard that sob! Misery, the feeling of misery being comparable to the "worm that does not die!"

"I do not have the right to touch my children's fortune," respond the rich. What will you leave them then, wretch, those whom you call audaciously your children? That wealth that you pretend to be theirs and that belongs no more to you than to them, at the moment you speak, it is tested in the furnace. Your money of blood and tears is tested by the fire that the children of the poor lack when it is freezing outside. He alone who has his Hands pierced has the right to speak of his children and the power to give them something after his death. You, you cannot bequeath to the so-called "yours" anything other than your shame for having wealth and your duty to restitute it.

Words spoken in vain, once again, I am greatly afraid, but words all the same of life and death. Even if it were in the desert, he who speaks amorously of poverty must be able to rouse the multitudes in order to hear him, like the Breath of the Lord that inspired life into Ezekiel's arid and dusty bones. Because Poverty is nothing less than the Spouse of the Son of God, and when his golden wedding party takes place, the Barefoot and the Famished will run from the extremities of the earth to be the witnesses thereof.

You know this, O Jewish Queen, Mother of

the Very Poor God whom the Bethlehem bourgeoisie would not receive, and who brought into the world, to lie upon the straw of animals, Your adorable Infant. You know what it cost him, only the *Veil* of that magnificent Spouse, whose hair of light has floated for twenty centuries now over all the graves of the Saints, from Orient to Occident. Better than anyone, You know also that Jesus is dead *for It*[62] *alone*. As for the Child's hatred for riches, only you could say that it is just as great as his Divinity even, and that that cannot be translated into any language.

I entrust You then with this book written by a poor man for the glory of Poverty. If bitterness should be found in it, You will mix in Your Sweetness, and if anger should be found in it, You will attenuate it with Your Sadness. But, do not forget, I am a contemporary of your Apparition on the Mountain of Tears.[63] I was placed, then, under Your Feet. In that capacity, Your Indignation and Your Seven Swords belong to me. The bronze chains that were seen on Your Shoulders, You left them for me as you were leaving, and behold sixty-three years have passed as I drag them through the world. It is their noise that importunes the cowards and the sleepers. If it is even possible anymore, make them into a roar of thunder to waken the rich finally – to Penitence or to Terror – O Star of Morning of the Poor, who "will laugh on the Last Day!"

*– Feast of the Annunciation, March 25, 1909.*

---

[62]It: Poverty.

[63]Mountain of Tears. A reference to La Salette.

# Other Books by the Publisher

*Fanchette's Pretty Little Foot*
by Restif de La Bretonne

*Je M'Accuse...*
by Léon Bloy

*My Hospitals & My Prisons*
by Paul Verlaine

*Salvation Through the Jews*
by Léon Bloy

*Words of a Demolitions Contractor*
by Léon Bloy

*Cellulely*
by Paul Verlaine

*Flowers of Bitumen*
by Émile Goudeau

*Songs for Her & Odes in Her Honor*
by Paul Verlaine

*On Huysmans' Tomb*
by Léon Bloy

*Ten Years a Bohemian*
by Émile Goudeau

*The Soul of Napoleon*
by Léon Bloy